From Fear
to Freedom

From Fear to Freedom

Choosing High Self-Esteem

Darlene Deer Truchses

FULCRUM, INC.
GOLDEN, COLORADO

Book Design by Jody Chapel, Cover to Cover Design
Cover Photograph by Wilken Photography, Denver, Colorado

Original edition published by New Options Publishing, Denver,
Colorado, in 1985 under the title *From Fear to Freedom: A Woman's
Handbook for High Self-Esteem*. All text and illustrations reprinted by
permission.

Library of Congress Cataloging-in-Publication Data

Truchses, Darlene Deer.
    From fear to freedom : choosing high self esteem / Darlene
Deer Truchses.
        p.   cm.
    Earlier ed. has subtitle: A woman's handbook for high
self-esteem.
    ISBN 1-55591-049-1
    1.   Women—United States—Psychology.   2. Self-respect.
3. Self-actualization (Psychology) I. Title.
HQ1206.T78   1989
155.6'33—dc20   89-7751
                                                         CIP

Fulcrum, Inc.
Golden, Colorado

To my children
Jenny, Amy, Colby and David
with love

Contents

Preface

This is an active book and a questioning book. As you read it, take time to formulate your own answers to the questions posed. After you are satisfied that you have your answers, read on and consider the options presented. Read the book slowly, or if you prefer, go through it quickly and then reread it. Some ideas require a second reading or experiential reinforcement before they sink in. Remember that any changes you attempt will occur gradually, and sometimes your only reinforcement will be how you feel about your new behavior.

You can also use the book as a resource for a support network you might want to start in your community. This material derives from numerous group discussion and private therapy sessions. Some of the women from these groups have formed alumnae groups that meet regularly to discuss new topics, reinforce behaviors, remind themselves of some understandings they may have forgotten, and gain fresh insights from a repeated discussion. Even women who are veterans of self-awareness groups tend to allow themselves to become caught in caretaker roles in the most nondomestic aspects of their lives.

The portrayals and case studies I have used are very real indeed, but I have altered some of the specifics, especially the names, to ensure confidentiality.

This is not a "how-to" book. I do not presume to be able to tell you how to lead your life. But you will discover that the many questions I ask here will guide you to the answers within you.

Use the book for understanding and growth. That is the goal.

Acknowledgments

The women who have participated through their sharing and questioning are the foundation of this book. We have learned from one another. I wish to thank Dick, my husband and co-therapist, for his vital support, assistance, trust and enthusiasm.

The revised edition is possible because of the enthusiastic response thousands of readers have given to the original edition of *From Fear to Freedom*. My sincere thanks to Pat Frederick and Fulcrum.

This book is about connecting; connecting brought the book into being.

Introduction

When I first started collecting this material, I had no idea it would become a book. I didn't even know I was collecting. My goal then was to survive! I wasn't in any physical danger, except for psychosomatic illnesses, but life was traumatic emotionally, with one change and challenge after another.

All of this personal turmoil was occurring at a time of huge societal turmoil for women. The feminist movement, with its questioning attitudes, provided me with the motivation to look at my responsibility for what was happening. I didn't want to blame others; it was too important to keep my relationships healthy and vital—the loving and caring ones as well as the painful ones.

Self-actualization became very important. I knew that for my life to be meaningful I had to combine self-actualization or personal power with the valuable characteristics of connecting—nurturing, caring, supporting, understanding and accepting. So I began to experiment. I didn't know how to combine personal power with connecting; the two seemed to be incompatible. There weren't any shoulds or musts as there had been for my earlier roles as daughter, wife, mother and woman. Then, the rules were well established. But they hadn't worked. What had happened?

So my investigation began, accidentally and somewhat haphazardly, and my goal changed from surviving to exploring, learning and making choices.

Several women in my new home town of Vail, Colorado, asked me to lead a group to look at how we had learned our role behaviors, our feelings and thoughts and our communication patterns. Each week they would suggest a topic for the next session; then I would research the topic and lead the discussion. They wanted to learn as much as I did, to understand, to explore, to question, to become aware, to make choices. They were exceptional women—as have been all the women who have joined me in my quest. After the first group, I realized the wealth of information I had. I formalized the outlines for the topics and started group sessions called "Women and Freedom."

In my private therapy practice, it was very apparent each day that low self-esteem was a major concern for most of the clients. They were facing a variety of crises and seemed to be well motivated toward change; they were ready to lead their lives in more meaningful ways. But how difficult it was for them to decide to give up low self-esteem for high self-esteem. At times, they appeared to cling to low self-worth, guarding their own negative feelings about themselves as if they were truths imprinted forever on their brains. More and more, it appeared that both men and women learn many ways to reinforce low self-worth, but not many ways to build high self-worth. For us women, especially, our learned roles and behaviors seem to be in conflict with our desire to achieve self-actualization, to lead our lives in meaningful ways and to acknowledge our own needs and wants.

Once again my goal changed. It had gone from surviving to exploring to reinforcing my high self-worth. My outlook broadened from a strictly personal interest to include a professional interest as I saw other women facing crises and decisions, experiencing conflicting feelings about personal growth and connecting.

Awareness, choice and freedom became the key concepts. Self-confidence and high self-worth are reinforced by being aware of our own feelings and behavior, by having knowledge of ourselves on a feeling level and comprehending the behavior options. Then we can choose. Then the responsibility becomes ours. We cannot try to give away that responsibility if our ultimate goal is to maintain high self-esteem and gain equality.

Freedom implies security in choosing one's options as clearly and objectively as possible, without blaming or condemning, without ignoring or being resentful, hurt or angry. We can no longer say, "It's his fault," "That's the way it has always been done," "My mother, father, children, boss, etc., are to blame for the way I am," "He made me angry," "If only this...," "If only that . . . ." It's important that we assume self-management and self-responsibility in order to evolve into the picture we have framed for ourselves.

The woman I will be tomorrow will probably be different from the woman I am today, because I can gain from today's experiences and understanding. There is no "real me." How stagnant and rigid I would be without change. My "me" is living my life in the present, learning from the past and planning for the future with a solid foundation of self-awareness, openness and, especially, self-confidence based on high self-worth.

There is no way to overestimate the importance of high self-worth. From that vantage point, we can learn to value ourselves and others, respect our rights and theirs and develop our own skills and talents. At the same time, we can cultivate and sustain meaningful, loving relationships and nurture and release our children, establishing models for them to appraise.

It is my hope that men, too, will benefit from the material presented here. The formula for high self-worth is the same for men and women. Perhaps learning about women's role behaviors will help men begin to comprehend their own role behaviors, and then to challenge those behaviors to see if they are working for them now.

The purpose of *From Fear to Freedom* is to help you, the reader, gain insight and understanding, to accept yourself and others and to forgive whenever possible. There are no "answers" or "right ways." The ways you choose and the answers you find are your own.

Premises

1. *Feelings* are feelings only. They are not to be judged as negative or positive, good or bad. *Behavior* can be judged, but all feelings are acceptable.
2. No one can *make* you feel glad, mad, sad or scared or any other feeling. You *choose* your reactions.
3. *Self-acquaintance* and *self-awareness* are quite different from selfishness.
4. *Assertiveness* builds and maintains relationships.
5. *High self-worth* is your most important decision.

The main goal for women is to give themselves the high regard, respect and caring that they customarily give to others. In this way, they will be able to realize their potential for creative connecting and fulfilling self-actualization.

1

....

The Subtle

(and Not So Subtle)

Put-Downs

What do you notice about someone you have just met? Eyes? Hair? Mouth? Hands? Nose? Smile? Clothes? When you think about your best friend, do you recall your friend's appearance, or rather that she or he is reliable? Friendly? Truthful? Humorous? It's interesting, isn't it, that when we first meet someone, we judge from appearances, but when we know someone better, we tend to put aside the first impressions about appearances and judge her or him on the basis of qualities and personality characteristics, in other words who she or he is.

Self-Assessment

Let's turn the questions around. Think about yourself. What are your personality characteristics? Are you

friendly? Quiet? Trustworthy? Sincere? Humorous?
Spontaneous? Are you someone you can count on? Do
you value yourself? Or do you even think about your
personal qualities? It may seem a bit embarrassing to
think of yourself favorably, to value yourself for who you
are, especially if you've been taught to be modest and to
value others before or above yourself.

Pretend that you are meeting yourself for the first
time. There you are, being introduced, extending your
hand and smiling at this new woman. Good grief! Her
eyes are too small and too close together. Her hair is too
curly. Her mouth is crooked and too thin. Her hands
are wrinkled and her nails are imperfect. Her smile is
okay, you guess. But she's too fat around the hips. And
her breasts are too big (or too small—there are only two
sizes). What an unacceptable woman she is (you are)!

Body Beautiful?

What do you really like about yourself physically?
Take a large piece of paper and three crayons. Or,
instead, simply imagine yourself doing this exercise.
Choose a neutral color, then a favorite color and then
a color you dislike. With the neutral color draw an
outline of yourself, front and back. With the color you
like, color in the parts of your body that are pleasing to
you. With the color you dislike, do the same for the parts
you would like to change. Think about your choices
before you read on.

It's incredible how many women have learned to
dislike their bodies. While some women do accept
themselves physically, most of us do not. Often, when
we use the word *too* we are viewing ourselves as unacceptable or different from the norm. We are very, very
quick to criticize ourselves. When you look into a mirror

do you ever consider giving at least equal time to praise yourself for the way you look? Most women will answer no. They can come up with criticisms infinitely. Seldom will a woman look at herself and say, "I feel good today," "I'm nifty" or "The most beautiful woman in the world slept in my bed last night."

Have you ever thought about what a difference it could have made if we had been encouraged as small children to accept our bodies, to learn to keep them healthy, relaxed and finely tuned? Perhaps the physical manifestations of stress would be reduced if children were taught relaxation exercises. Recent studies indicate that practicing relaxation results in enhanced creativity, increased productivity and decreased anxiety.

But, instead, both physical and intellectual competition is encouraged. "Be better." "Get all A's." "Be on the ski team or the soccer team." We continue to reinforce our children for *what they do* instead of for *who they are.*

Many of you were encouraged in this same way, and you didn't learn to value yourself—only to value your achievements. That, coupled with negative opinions of yourself physically, is one of the reasons your self-esteem didn't flourish.

Competitiveness

We've been taught to be modest and self-effacing. Yet, at the same time, we're supposed to be as beautiful as possible and competitive with one another. We are taught a conflict.

We learn to compete with one another physically. When you are in a group of people, do you occasionally or even often appraise the other women? When you are with another couple, what are your thoughts? Do you notice your friend's appearance when you are meeting for lunch? Do you rate yourself? There is little doubt that competitiveness in terms of beauty alone is re-inforced.

Whenever I think about competitiveness, I think first of sports. In order to be good at an individual or team sport, one must have not only skill but also faith in oneself. Perhaps that's a good basic definition of high self-esteem: *primarily, having faith and trust in oneself and one's characteristics; and sometimes, secondarily, having this faith and trust reinforced by skill and success and others' praise.* But too often, although we have learned to be competitive, we haven't learned to have faith in our-selves or to value ourselves for *who* we are, for the per-sonal qualities that make us unique. Instead we learn to value ourselves for *what* we do. I've met many women who have accomplished a lot so far as professional achievements are concerned, the things by which soci-ety mistakenly measures self-worth. But, at the same time, they feel bad about themselves. They have learned to value themselves for what they do and ignore who they are.

Who vs. What

Do you know *who* you are? Or do you continue to identify yourself by *what* you do?

When I asked Darcey, an extremely active mother, student and working professional who she is, she could not answer. She said she had never thought about who, only what. Then I asked her to tell me why she liked her best friend. She was able to do that in glowing terms: kind, patient, fun, intelligent, pretty, compassionate, considerate, thoughtful. The next step was for Darcey to tell me why her friend liked her. Although she quickly saw my point, she struggled with valuing herself in the same way as when I asked her about her friend. This is the exercise you can do yourself, as suggested at the start of this chapter. It's very important that you know *who you are* because without *who you are* there would be no *what you do.*

Put-Downs from the Past

How have we learned to judge ourselves? In the earliest years we were very dependent upon other people's influences and opinions, especially those of our parents or others with whom we lived. If we were encouraged to think well of ourselves, we generally would, but all too often others were unthinking or perhaps unaware of what message a child can perceive. "You're smart, your sister is beautiful," "You're the skinniest kid in town," "You're the only one in the family who has to be taken to the chubby department"—or, when you're seven and need glasses, "Isn't that too bad?"

Then when you're a bit older and can discriminate between your own likes and dislikes about physical appearances, you're told that "you're going to have hips just like Aunt Jane." You think about Aunt Jane's hips and you believe all hope is lost. Or your mother is frustrated by constantly having to comb your stubborn hair and tells you that "there's no style that works."

Stop and think a minute about messages you received as a child. Were they positive? Did they help you feel good about yourself? Or were they harmful?

Ostracism and Teasing

Children usually team up with children with whom they are similar, excluding any child who seems to be "different." If you were the one who was ostracized, you probably experienced very early the pain of rejection and may have come to view yourself unfavorably. If you were in with the crowd, you may not have fared much better, because you might have felt the pressure to continue to be accepted, the agony of being even temporarily cut out. And then you wondered, "What is wrong with me?"

Another way children learn nonacceptance is by being teased. There is a lot of argument in favor of teasing. Some people believe that teasing is an important part of childhood, a way to learn to adapt and to desensitize. If you're the teaser, you can even feel powerful. Most likely you did not take teasing seriously because it can have a humorous side. Teasing can be reciprocated so that it becomes a game of skill requiring fast thinking and quick wit.

The argument supporting teasing presented most frequently is that you tease only the people you care about. But I wonder if teasing is really just a socially accepted expression of aggression. I'm certainly not convinced it's a high self-esteem form of communication. The remarks can be cutting, the nicknames can be debasing and the words can disguise hidden anger.

Among children, teasing is often based on names. Mary is contrary. Jeannie is a meany. Sally is silly. All too often children will believe that whatever they are teased about is not okay. They view teasing as mean and not nice. They get the impression that it would be better if they were different from who they actually are. Teasing makes them feel uncomfortable and unacceptable. Were you called a nickname as a child? Porky? Skinny? Four eyes? Peachy? Cutie? Shorty? Perhaps you were teased because of physical characteristics that you could do nothing about. This is another prevalent childhood teasing pattern. A good friend of mine was born with a deviated septum; as a result, one of his nostrils was slightly flattened. His classmates nicknamed him "Nutty Nostrils."

The opinions that we have of ourselves as children are frequently both lasting and negative. A skinny little girl may have a hard time as a grown woman not thinking of herself as too thin, even though she may be quite shapely. More often, when a plump little girl grows into a woman, she will see in her mirror an overweight woman, even though her weight is normal. Without examination these childhood images can follow a woman for a lifetime.

Little girls are taught incredible paradoxes. Be beautiful, but also be modest and self-effacing. Be outstanding, but not so outstanding that others feel bad. Don't get upset by teasing, even though it hurts. Remember, good little girls don't get angry.

Hangovers from the Teen Years

Then there are the teen years. Can you remember calling your best friend to see what she was planning to wear to school? Heaven forbid that you should look different! Of course, you were supposed to stand out; who would pay attention to you if you didn't? But you might also have been fearful of standing out too much. Then you could be thought of as snobbish or stuck-up. You probably didn't give the whole conflict a lot of thought. You were just uncomfortable. Now, however, you can look back and realize that at the time you were experiencing an uneasiness with yourself—an uneasiness that you may have brought to the present.

During your teens you might have started to read fashion magazines. Then the specter of "the perfect woman" emerges. The boldface type on the cover of a fashion magazine states, "THIS IS THE YEAR TO BE YOUNG, THIN AND HEALTHY." Such magazines can be very destructive to us, especially if we compare ourselves to the way the models look and decide that that is the way we are supposed to look.

Do you compare yourself unfavorably to some standard of perfection? Do you see a picture of a woman you admire and then judge yourself as coming up short? If you do, you aren't being fair to yourself. An alternative response is for you to use the pictures as guides. If you like someone's style, don't copy it; instead, choose from it what you can adapt to your own style. We learn our own particular styles by experimenting, not by criticizing and rejecting our own persons.

A young woman in one of my groups responded with tears to the question, "Do you think you are attractive?" She was responding to a lifetime of comparing herself with others and underestimating herself. In reality her features resemble those of some of the more outstanding models and actresses. Over the weeks of the discussions, her fellow group members could actually see the change in her. As she reinforced her high self-esteem, she became able to appreciate her uniqueness, her singular beauty. By her own admission, she feels proud.

Behavior Labels

In our society, parenting is frequently done by using guilt, shame and fear. We forget to separate children from their behavior and instead judge the child by her or his behavior. An object is accidentally broken: "You're bad." Milk is spilled: "Stupid kid." A tired child cries: "Spoiled" or "Brat." You are "Worthless," "Useless,"

"Naughty." Were you labeled like this?

Occasionally, parental or grandparental motives, even though well intentioned, can have quite destructive results. Ginny, an accomplished professional woman, related that as a young child she was continually compared with other children. When she would come home with an extremely good report card, she would be asked by her grandmother, "Did anyone do better?" If the answer was yes, then she was told, "You can do better; you can be best." Similar questions were asked about "prettier" and "more popular." Ginny thought of herself as always lacking, even though she tried hard. The irony is that trying hard helped her become accomplished, but she didn't believe in herself and continued to harbor a strong anger toward her grandmother, until she finally realized that her childhood impression of herself was no longer relevant.

Granted, there are behaviors that are unacceptable. There are things we don't want our children to do, but we can have greater success telling a child what we want instead of what we don't want. Children want and are very dependent upon acceptance. A small child will respond to a positive directive and will feel good about parental pleasure and reinforcement. A child who feels good about herself or himself will be open to nurturing, caring and teaching.

Were you a child who was parented with guilt, shame and fear? If you were, you suffered from self-worth malnutrition. Were you rewarded or punished for *what* you did instead of appreciated for *who* you are?

Continuing the Put-Down Legacy

If you aren't the way you believe you should be, do you turn your back on yourself? Do you turn yourself inside out? If you aren't "in the league of looking voluptuous and soft and sensual and pussy-catty, sort of" (the words of a woman in one of the groups), do you go the other way? Do you dress to hide and fade into the crowd? Do you think makeup is silly or useless? In other words, do you forfeit the game? Whenever I hear a woman state, "I don't like other women because they're catty, or they talk only about babies or the pain they experienced having them, or the awfulness of house-keeping," I always wonder about that woman's view of herself. Although there may be some truth in the statements, generally what the woman is really saying is, "I don't want to compete with other women; I don't like myself enough."

Hiding Out

Challenge yourself. Are you hiding out? You can hide out in a variety of ways. You can reject the more common values society uses for attractiveness by being very fat or very thin. You can be almost invisible in your plainness or so outlandish you are beyond compare. Don't kid yourself that you're succeeding in your game. You're still reacting to a set of standards in much the same way a rebellious child does. You cling to a poor physical image to avoid competing. If you recognize yourself in this description and choose to look squarely at your opinion of yourself, you're on the road to freedom. A free woman moves independently, picking and choosing from an endless variety of samples.

Buying Madison Avenue's Message

Another way we learn to see ourselves as deficient is by buying the messages presented in advertising. Consider all the advertised products we are told we require to be acceptable. Toothpaste and deodorant may be a must, but do we really need vaginal douches that deodorize? Lipstick that gleams? Fingernails that attract his attention? Would I be more desired by my mate or lover if I wore uplifting bras—or the separating variety? Would I be L-I-B-E-R-A-T-E-D if I smoked a certain kind of cigarette? Would my life be happier if I drank light beer, which would make me thinner and, therefore, more acceptable?

The major portion of advertising is designed to create a belief of deficiency or need. We are encouraged to look at how we would be better if we purchased a certain product—which implies that without the product we must somehow be less. And so it goes. We view ourselves as lacking.

Despite the public's increased awareness of advertising's role stereotypes, many of the traditional male and female roles are still emphasized through advertising. How many dishwashing detergent ads feature men's hands?

Advertising messages are often degrading to a woman's image of herself as an intelligent person capable of taking care of herself. However, there does appear to be a movement afoot in the advertising world that indicates that some advertisers are trying to change their ways. The talk now is of the "fully dimensional woman," the "cross-over woman" and the return to more traditional values combining home, family and job.[1] But don't relax. Even these messages could try to incite guilt because we aren't the *new* way we should be.

In sum, be aware of what you are hearing and reading so that you can detect messages of low self-worth and sexism. They continue to creep in, especially in advertising.

Succumbing to the Age Myth

A subject that is fertile ground for the put-down is *aging*. We're going downhill and there's no way to stop it. Youth (so the saying goes) is fleeting. If we aren't already "older," we can foresee breasts that droop from nursing and gravity, hips that are no longer narrow and firm, hair that is graying and chins that sag. In extreme cases of concern about the physical ravages of aging, women can give themselves what I call "aging psychosis"—a preoccupation unaddressed by textbooks, but seemingly prevalent. A psychosis is defined as *any severe mental disorder, with or without organic damage, characterized by deterioration of normal intellectual and social functioning and by partial or complete withdrawal from reality.*[2] That certainly sounds like an accurate description of how many women view growing older. They look at aging as deterioration and loss.

Well, you aren't required to view growing older in those ways. No matter what your age is now, you can begin to believe that your beauty, vitality, interest, intellect and wisdom can grow with the years and be greatly enhanced by your self-awareness and willingness to discover. In *Pathfinders*, Gail Sheehy describes at some length the advantages of being older.[3]

Rising Up from the Put-Down

By now you can begin to understand how women have absorbed, unquestioningly, many indirect and direct put-down messages that have contributed to their underrating themselves. If you are one of these women, there are some important things to consider that may help you change your opinions.

1. Don't allow yourself the useless indulgence of *yearning.* Yearning, defined quite simply, is *desiring, without action, to be different.* In order to change, it's important that you achieve self-management and decide what you want to do and how you want to be. Yearning takes time and energy that could be spent much more productively doing whatever it is you decide to do. Yearning also continues to reinforce the notion that you are "not okay."

2. Be more *aware.* Be open to options and suggestions. Allow your mind to wander and determine how you might have absorbed lessons that contributed to your not accepting yourself and your consequent low self-esteem. Even though the words may have been different, the lessons you learned might have been quite similar.

3. Put aside *blaming.* One school of thought contends that understanding the past tends to help people stay stuck. That would be true if you allowed yourself to understand why you behave as you do but did nothing to comprehend how you are bringing your well-learned behaviors and opinions into the present. If you allow that to happen, you are reinforcing yourself as a powerless victim.

4. As you read the information and shared insights in this book, reflect on what you learned in your past and what is unique for you. *Discuss* your beliefs and your opinions with other people. Learn from them.

5. Allow yourself the pleasure of *flexibility.* Flexibility enhances high self-worth. Make choices about what is acceptable, what you want to discard and what you want to change. Focus on high self-worth. Sometimes we regard high self-worth almost like a town in the next state, or even across the country:

High Self-Worth
153 Miles

We regard it as a destination to be achieved, much as we would drive to another city. We may lose our way because of other people's opinions of how we should be. We may even lose the original road map because we change our goals. Our car could break down in minor or major ways because we suffer accidents or illnesses and losses through separation or death. Our companions could decide to ride with someone else because they divorce or move away. They might go on without us because their goals are different from ours.

The point is that we often view high self-worth as a goal to be achieved, something to work for. *Instead high self-worth is a decision you make. You can decide right now that you have high self-worth and then you learn the behaviors to reinforce your decision.* Please reread the last two sentences because they are a basic understanding. High self-worth is the fuel that moves us from childhood to maturity.

Be kind to yourself. Pay attention to how you are feeling. Give some thought to the whys. Make choices and decisions. Initiate change. Manage instead of control. Look for your options—they are your solutions.

Notes

1. *The Wall Street Journal,* October 28, 1982, p. 33.
2. William Morris, ed., *The American Heritage Dictionary of the English Language* (Boston: Houghton Mifflin Co., 1969).
3. Gail Sheehy, *Pathfinders* (New York: William Morrow & Co., 1981), pp. 218-232.

2

The Caught Caretaker

"If you don't do your sons' laundry, how do they know you love them?" a woman asked me during a group discussion on caretaking. The question exemplifies the extent to which some women are deeply caught up in, even enslaved by, the confusing role of caretaker.

Have you ever thought of caretaker as a role? What duties does it include? What does *caretaker* mean? Think carefully before you answer. Is caretaker a role unto itself, or is it a component of *all* your roles?

Roles Caretakers Play
What are your roles? Take a pencil and paper and in the middle of the paper, draw a circle with the word *me* in the center. From this circle, draw lines outward.

Allow space for lots of lines. At the end of each line, draw another circle. In each outer circle, write a role you fulfill, daily or infrequently, such as wife, daughter, friend, sister-in-law, artist, lover, chef, chauffeur, doctor, secretary, mother, church member, tennis player— all the different roles you can think of.

Surprised at the number of different roles you have? There could be another surprise, however. Look at the roles carefully. For each one, write a brief job description, one or two sentences that occur to you quickly. Are caretaking duties apparent in most of your roles?

Caretaking Labels

Now, explore a little farther afield from your roles and ask yourself some questions about labels given to women. Go slowly and thoughtfully, and think about your answers.

What's "feminine"? What's "ladylike"? What's "motherly"? In a roomful of women, you'll get many different answers. There's no set definition for any of those labels. Of course, Webster's dictionary has definitions, but each woman has her own.

However, there are some commonalities. Words frequently used to describe a feminine, ladylike, motherly woman include *delicate, caring, nurturing, graceful, composed, gracious, giving, comforting, dainty, supportive, frilly, compassionate, gentle, happy, soft, charming, dignified, worrying, tender, passive, helping*. If you have any other words, add them to the list. Now check carefully for the implication of caretaking in all the words. Incredible, isn't it? Even in words such as *gracious*, caretaking plays a part.

Caretaking in the Professional World

We aren't finished investigating yet. What are the traditional female professions? The usual list starts with teacher or nurse. Then come social worker, secretary, waitress, flight attendant, clerk, psychologist. Today we can also include physician and lawyer. Again, think about the job descriptions for these professions. Each one has some kind of service orientation and frequently, again, a caretaking component.

Those of you who are saying, "But that's all changing now" have an important point. According to a recent study by the Rand Corporation, 25 percent of all new graduates in law, medicine and business are women, compared to .05 percent twenty years ago; and from 1980 to 1986, wages of all working women increased from 60 percent to 65 percent of men's wages. The study made a conservative estimate that women would possibly make 80 percent of men's wages by the year 2000. However, the caretaking professions have been traditionally low paying. Compare a male social worker to a male professional athlete, for example. You might often hear the remark, "That's good pay for a woman." Have you ever heard, "That's good pay for a man"?

Go further with your investigation.

The Caretaker's Creed: Thee before Me

When someone asks you who's the most important person in your life, I hope you can truthfully answer "me." But if you discover you're thinking "my husband" or "my children," or some other important person or persons, you are probably caught by the caretaking definitions of yourself that you discovered when you did the exercises at the beginning of the chapter. If you haven't already acknowledged that you are the most important person in your life, it's necessary that you do so now.

Does admitting that you are the most important person in your life seem selfish, self-centered, thoughtless or egotistical? Those are the characteristics women usually mention immediately. Of course, that's what we have been taught. As caretakers, we have to take care of others first; then, at some later point, we turn to ourselves. But certainly we do not put ourselves first.

Allow yourself to believe that it's okay for each person, female or male, to take care of herself or himself first. (Men have no problem with this.) Women have been taught that it's not okay. By acknowledging that you are the top woman on your own totem pole, you will be more open to your feelings, the motivators for your thoughts and behavior. You will be more aware and understanding and more capable of learning new, direct and honest behaviors. This important acknowledgment does not mean you are selfish, self-centered, thoughtless or egotistical. You'll be able to comprehend, as you read later chapters, how women who do not freely acknowledge their own importance have learned to be manipulative while appearing passive, to inhibit themselves sexually and to deny themselves the full range of self-acquaintance and self-actualization.

Caretaking: Caught or Free

As we continue to examine the caretaker role, a confusing contradiction emerges. It appears that caretaking may actually be destructive. Many women have difficulty understanding the destructive aspect of the caretaking role: that they may become caught in the role rather than freely choose it.

The difference between being caught in the caretaker's role and being free in the same role is very subtle. Quite simply stated, *being free in the role is understanding and believing that you have a* choice *to be nurturing, caring, supporting, understanding and accepting when you* choose *and to whom you* choose; *being caught in the role is believing that you* must *be nurturing, caring, supporting, understanding and accepting to all persons all of the time.*

Certainly there is nothing wrong with being nurturing, caring, supporting, understanding and accepting. Those are important characteristics that can improve the quality of life for everyone. They are values by which we can reinforce ourselves for *who we are.*

But why do so many of us buy into the extreme belief that we must be nurturing, caring, supporting, understanding and accepting to all persons all of the time? Why do we become caught caretakers? The answer is simple: We have been carefully taught (see Chapter 1) that *who we are* (our characteristics) is less important than *what we do* (our duties), so we believe that we must *do*, that is, be caretaking.

Self-Definitions

Each of us has a self-definition. It's complex because our self-definition extends beyond how we define ourselves to include how we would like others to define us. The ways we define ourselves include judging ourselves—poor, good, better, best—on a variety of characteristics and abilities that go from physical attributes to emotional stability to professional achievement. Most of us want other people to think well of us, possibly love us, so we go about trying to achieve that goal, even when we judge ourselves very harshly. We want to be connected with others and approved by them.

When our self-esteem is low, we believe we must work hard to achieve others' admiration and love. We substitute our personal characteristics (who we are) for our achievements and responsibilities (what we do). We become dependent upon outside approval. We do not look inward; we do not value ourselves. We are not our own "best friend." Remember Darcey and the *who* exercise in Chapter 1? For an extremely valuable aid for learning self-acceptance, read *How to Be Your Own Best Friend* by Mildred Newman and Bernard Berkowitz, with Jean Owen.[1]

Caretaker as Controller

If you don't understand your high self-value, you will try, in a caught caretaker role, to be central to others' functioning. You will attempt to manage other people's lives. You will try to exercise indirect power. You will be fearful that others will learn to be autonomous or independent, because then you would not be necessary in their lives. The caught caretaker role is a way to pat yourself on the back because you will perceive yourself as important. You will try to control others.

The idea of controlling is repulsive to some women. They are so reluctant to view themselves as controlling that they will reject any suggestion of the possibility. However, the truth is that a woman (or man) caught in the old definition of the caretaker role does try to control others. Since she believes she must be nurturing, caring, supporting, understanding and accepting to all persons all of the time, she will be trapped by that belief. She will not allow herself to directly acknowledge herself as the most important person in her life.

At the same time she is doing for others, she is dependent upon them for their love and approval. Not recognizing that she is lovable because of who she is (her attitudes and personal characteristics), she will undervalue herself, substituting her duties, responsibilities and achievements as ways to gain recognition, depending on the responses of those around her. Their responses need to be as she requires them to be: "loving husband," "obedient daughter," "successful son," "loyal friend." She will then be able to label herself a "good wife," "effective mother" or "lovable friend." These labels become her self-definitions, replacing her characteristics. As women have learned to be controlling, they have learned powerlessness, subservience, other-directedness and under-self-valuing. The whole situation is an incredible paradox, yet society supports the unachievable effort.

Self-Actualization and Connecting

While the paradox of the controlling-powerless caretaker sounds terribly discouraging, there are new options. First, let's define *connecting* and *self-actualization*. Quite simply, connecting means relating to others, enabling ourselves and them to experience personal enrichment through the relationship. Self-actualization is a concept advanced by Abraham Maslow, a psychologist who studied successful people. Self-actualizers are essentially self-directed and self-supported and recognize their own needs and wants. They live primarily in the present, with a meaningful relationship to the past and future. They are sensitive to others' approval and love, but are not dependent upon others. They are aware of their own feelings. They are accepting and flexible, not rigid in adherence to social pressures. They are capable of close and loving relationships. Reread the definition so you understand that self-actualization is not selfish, self-centered, thoughtless or egotistical.

Connecting. Self-actualization. The two concepts don't sound opposing, do they? They aren't. But women often confuse them because they confuse attitudes and duties.

Think back to the beginning of this chapter. Reflect upon your awareness of how women's roles, labels and professions are traditionally laced with caretaking. Now, ask yourself these questions:

1. How do I define myself?
2. How do I want others to define me?
3. How do I try to gain approval and love?
4. Do I have my caretaker attitudes confused with caretaker duties?
5. Do I count on the duties to reflect my attitudes?
6. Do I count on the duties to gain the love and approval I want?
7. Do I count on the duties to represent my approval and love for others?
8. Do I compromise myself (my feelings, opinions and desires) in order to be approved or in order to be approving?
9. Do I feel resentment, anger and guilt more than I like to admit?
10. Am I fearful that I cannot be both connecting and self-actualizing?

As you formulate answers to the questions, remember that as human beings we have extremely complex behaviors and interactions. There is never a single reason why we act as we do, although frequently it may look that way. Don't allow yourself to be too quickly assured that if you understand your caretaker role, you'll have all the answers. However, understanding your caretaker role *is* extremely valuable, and you'll comprehend how the caretaker role infiltrates your behavior, beliefs and attitudes.

Your Self-Definition

Starting with the first question, how do you define yourself? As pretty or attractive? Is my body okay or does it need improvement? Am I sexy? A plain Jane? Do I identify myself with any famous woman? If so, which of her qualities or characteristics do I try to adopt? What are my important personality characteristics? Patience? Kindness? Thoughtfulness? Am I quick-tempered? Worthy? Impulsive? Am I a loser? A winner? Courageous? Creative?

Perhaps these questions can help you devise your self-definition. Most of us do not want to think too poorly of ourselves, so we may avoid a lot of the critical observations. That's good. Pay close attention if you discover that you have a tendency to define yourself critically. If you are doing that, you are essentially reinforcing low self-esteem. Allow your self-definition to be accepting rather than rejecting. By defining yourself in approving ways, you will reinforce your decision to enjoy high self-worth.

Don't underestimate the importance of your self-definition. We carry out our definitions in our lives. If we view ourselves as losers, for example, we set up situations in which we lose. Winners generally win, and when they don't (because they take risks that don't always work out) they still gain in some fashion from the experience. When we view ourselves primarily as caretakers, we try to carry out that definition.

Understanding your self-definition will help you comprehend some of your familiar behavior patterns. I'm not implying that understanding that definition will enable you to handle complex behaviors such as choosing repeatedly to marry an alcoholic or an abuser, but comprehending how you define yourself is a good beginning.

Others' Definition of You

How do you want others to define you? Sometimes the ways we define ourselves are the ways we want others to see us. Generally we want others to approve of us, even though we ourselves may be self-disapproving. When we care too much what others think of us, we may underrate our own self-acceptance and become extremely dependent upon others' approval.

Have you ever known someone, or are *you* someone, who requires practically constant reinforcement? Talk about the bottomless pit—pretty soon you or others are worn out! No matter what is said, it is either not enough, not believed or both. Self-actualizers believe in themselves. They trust themselves. They understand their personal rights. Of course, they have significant mentors or peers, important persons whose approval they seek, but they are not dependent upon that approval.

Allowing ourselves to be almost totally dependent on others' approval is a very risky business. Each of us has her or his own context. Sometimes our friends and family are so involved with what is happening to them that they're too busy to be concerned with what is going on with us. Being dependent upon others' approval means, in a sense, subjecting ourselves to the winds of fate. People move, they become involved in their own things, they choose others. These events do not mean that there is something wrong with us, but if we allow ourselves to be overly dependent on others' definitions of us, we set the stage for disappointment and reinforce low self-esteem.

Gaining Approval and Love

How do you try to gain approval and love? There certainly is no debate that approval and love are important to each of us. Essentially, that's what connecting is all about. There are even certain philosophies that view us as part of a whole, with no apparent beginnings or endings, only connections.

Sometimes people work hard to deny any desire for others' approval and love. We say these people are defensive or not vulnerable. Not being vulnerable can be a way of protecting ourselves—of helping ourselves through difficult times when we've experienced rejection or death. We think that we can't handle the pain again so we develop a *defensive self-reliance*, telling ourselves that we do not need anyone, which helps us over the hard spots by denying our desire for approval and love. Hopefully, the defensive self-reliance is temporary, because without vulnerability, we do not allow ourselves to risk the pleasures of connecting.

The case for gaining approval and love is well established. So how do you go about the task?

Perhaps you try by doing for others. While that sounds innocent enough on the surface, what does it really mean? Saying yes when you want to say no? Working harder than your co-workers? Denying your own priorities in favor of others' priorities? Working yourself into a frenzy? Being a superwoman? A supermom? For many women, doing things for others never ends—maybe if you do enough, you'll be loved and approved. What a myth—sometimes we even do for people who don't want it!

Attitudes and Duties

You are probably beginning to comprehend that it is very easy to confuse attitudes with duties. We've already established that a woman is taught caretaking. As a little girl, she learns to take care of her brothers and sisters or her father and mother and frequently the younger children at school. She learns to do housekeeping chores and she is presented with homemaking toys. She's taught that these chores are important because they provide comfort for others. They represent caring.

As a teenager, the caretaker's duties continue. In addition to whatever she may be doing at home or church or school, she may help someone with homework, write a term paper for a friend, allow someone to use her notes or look over her shoulder at her answers.

Professionally, a woman is encouraged toward the helping professions. Sometimes she is directly discouraged from seeking other professions because of a potential conflict with marriage and family. She will play "the waiting game," waiting for fulfillment as a caretaking wife and mother.

The confusion about duties and attitudes continues and grows. Caretaking activities expand like dandelions in the yard. Homes must be cared for, laundry done, meals prepared, babies fed, meetings attended and budgets balanced. Soon a woman begins to count on the duties to reflect her attitudes.

I hope that, in addition to the caretaking duties themselves, you also learned as a young girl that nurturing, caring, supporting, understanding and accepting are extremely important attitudes. They are the attitudes that give strength to life and encourage love and vitality. However, the confusion sets in when you begin to believe that what you *do*, especially for others, represents how you *feel* about them. Unfortunately, this is what many of us have been taught.

Men have received essentially the same kind of lesson, but they have traditionally been taught to be providers instead of caretakers. The resulting equation for a man in a relationship has therefore been *I provide = You caretake me*, as opposed to the woman's equation, *I caretake you = You provide*. Although the situation is gradually changing, the point is that men and women both count on their duties to reflect their attitudes.

Counting on Duties for Love and Approval

Although you may acknowledge that the caretaker *attitudes* are extremely important to you, you have probably also decided that the *duties* aren't all that important. Like a lot of women, you may be trying to establish a new pattern at home: the division of tasks. The totally surprising thing, however, is that you may discover you're having difficulty relinquishing those tasks to others! Is that because you count on duties to gain the love and approval you want?

Now it's time for some serious introspection. Do you ask your mate or family to help with the housework? Does your husband babysit? Do you say "thank you" for household tasks that others perform? Do you experience a twinge of guilt when you read the paper while someone else does the dishes?

Answer honestly. Once in a while, a woman can answer the above questions with the understanding that housework is housework, not woman's work. A

man can be a father instead of a babysitter. Others enjoy
the home, it's theirs, and consequently it is their responsibility as much as it is yours. And, finally, tasks can
be divided so that everyone can enjoy relaxation time—
not just men and children.

The answer that women frequently give, however, is
that although they have an intellectual *understanding* of
the behavior they want to change, their *feelings* get in the
way of carrying out the new behavior.

For example, when you describe yourself as "honest," you will probably go to great lengths to carry out
the opinion of yourself for your own integrity and for
others' trust. Honesty becomes a part of you. For women,
"caregiving" is a description. We're to be nurturing, caring, loving, accepting, supporting, understanding and
patient. Individually we may not have chosen caregiver
as a description, but society has chosen it for women col-
lectively. The role, as we've illustrated, is taught and
reinforced. The behavior and thoughts and feelings are
circular.

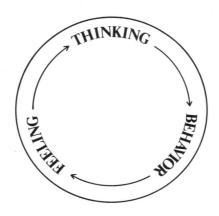

We can't readily separate them. It's very difficult to give up the duties or behavior because of our feelings of guilt. Therefore, when you ask yourself whether you count on the duties to represent your approval and love for others, you can begin to see that you might, if this is what you've been taught.

So how do you challenge yourself to change, if you decide you want to begin to do things differently?

You question the duties. You challenge the learned behavior. Does doing my sons' laundry really illustrate my love for them? How are housekeeping chores an example of my love and approval for others? Does preparing a gourmet meal show my family or mate I care about them? How does belonging to four PTAs (I once had four children in four different schools) illustrate my love for my children? When I stay overtime, with no extra pay, does my employer interpret it as my approval of her or him? Does baking cookies at Christmas or coloring Easter eggs or hand sewing Halloween costumes demonstrate my approval and love? (One of the women labeled this behavior "the dog and pony act.") When I say yes but I want to say no, does my friend know I care?

Make up your own lists and question yourself. That's the way you begin to comprehend what changes you want to make.

Compromising Oneself for Approval

Do you compromise yourself (your feelings and desires) in order to be approved of or in order to be approving? How many times have you held back, counted to ten, held your tongue, controlled yourself or swallowed your anger? How often do you change your mind in order to be agreeable? Maybe that's one clue to understanding why women are labeled "changeable." Do you frequently answer, "I don't care" or "I don't know" when you really do? Are you the peacemaker in your family, absorbing others' feelings, behavior and reactions? Are you hesitant to return a purchase you've decided you don't want?

If you answered "often" or "yes" to most or all of the above questions, know that you're not the only one. These are behaviors many women have been taught, and they are constantly reinforced. It's a mistake to come down on yourself because you behave in ways that you may now be questioning. Instead, remember that behavior is learned and what you've learned, you can unlearn or relearn. That's what progress and growth are all about. Use your high self-esteem as the fuel.

Resentment, Anger and Guilt

Do you feel resentment, anger and guilt more than you like to admit? It's quite incredible when you realize how women are instructed in "feminine" behaviors and feelings. Refer back briefly to the definitions of *feminine, ladylike* and *motherly* earlier in this chapter. Do you see any words that indicate our ability to experience human feelings, except, of course, *love, joy, pride* (in others), *guilt, grief* and *fear?*

We women tend to believe that we aren't supposed to feel resentment and anger, although guilt and fear are okay. After all, how can we be caregiving when we feel angry or resentful?

On the other hand, how can we feel otherwise when we lead our lives in so many denying ways—denying our own feelings, opinions and desires? We often rush in too quickly to save, rescue, make peace and provide. On the rare occasions when we do put ourselves in first place by being assertive, we feel guilty. But, of course, feeling guilty is okay because then we pay the price of doing or feeling something that was direct and honest for us.

Guilt is a complex feeling. Since it is a feeling common to women, you're probably already quite familiar with it, although perhaps you don't understand it very well.

I call guilt the token feeling, like tokens or money. When we do something (behavior) that is contrary to a belief, principle or feeling we have, we pay for that behavior by feeling guilty.

Women feel guilty very easily. When we question our learned roles enough to change our behavior, frequently the first feeling response is guilt, not self-congratulations that we have decided to effect the change. It's guilt, because we are doing something differently— in other words, not the way we've been taught.

Fear

Are you fearful that you cannot be both connecting and self-actualizing because you have perceived them to be incompatible? If you respond yes, it's important to explore the origin and basis of your fears.

The truth is that we do have real fears that we cannot, or perhaps should not, be both connecting and self-actualizing. This is especially true when we limit the definition of connecting to the duties of caught caretaking.

What are some of those fears? One might be the fear of loneliness. Another is the fear of power. A possible third is the fear of failure. In addition, we have learned we must have a relationship in order to be okay. We haven't learned to trust ourselves enough to test our abilities, so we do our "duty." It's important to consider all of your fears together. Then ask yourself if your fears are actually all fears of loss.

Remember the phrase, "It's lonely at the top"? What it implies is that power increases loneliness. For women, the response to the word *power* is varied.

Some don't like the word because they believe it implies hardness, victimizing people, insensitivity and manipulation. Power has been defined as *unfeminine.* When the descriptions are taken to an extreme, powerful women are not good lovers! Women are not supposed to be powerful; they are supposed to be caretakers.

However, a certain number of women will grasp onto power. For them it means a way to get even. They have felt powerless too long and they want to impose their will. They are the women who will try to attach blame for their feelings of inadequacy on others, mainly mothers and men. They reinforce the definition of *power* as dominance, aggressiveness and insensitivity.

Sometimes the resistance to power lies in a belief that power means male power. What is your definition of *male power?* It is like trying to define *feminine, ladylike* and *motherly*—there is no set definition. Each of us will use our fathers, brothers, husbands, lovers, male employers or male associates as models to help shape our definitions. That helps explain why male power can be unacceptable and scary or quite acceptable and desirable.

The catch for women seems to lie in the association of power and loneliness. No one really wants to be lonely (alone, maybe, but not lonely). Women will resist power or authority because they believe they will be lonely and therefore experience loss.

I'd like to explore another option for the definition of *power*. When I speak of power, I mean a *personal power* that includes our feelings of high self-worth, a trust in and regard for oneself, plus an ability to extend trust and regard to our family, friends and associates. It includes our ability to examine and become well acquainted with ourselves.

Personal power does *not* mean domineering, autocratic, self-serving—in other words, aggressive—behavior. It does include knowing self-management skills and being able to make decisions. It includes behaving assertively and learning the techniques of assertive interactions.

Does that sound like a pathway to loneliness? Certainly not. First, feeling personally powerful can help women develop peer relationships. Second, it can enable them to enhance their parenting because their interactions with their children will be clearer, more direct and honest. They can serve as models for their children. Modeling is a very important way children learn. Third, professional women who feel personal power will see themselves as equals, secure in their skills and expertise. They will not have to "try harder." That doesn't mean they can allow themselves to relax their efforts. Instead, it means women can believe in themselves and give up all the proving they do. Then their skills can be applied productively to achievements and leadership.

I am not saying that enjoying personal power can eliminate our fears of loneliness, loss and rejection. Loss and rejection are real events that human beings endure. The danger resides in our *allowing the fears of loss to be dominant* so that we shape our behavior to try to avoid being lonely or losing or feeling rejection. What we may actually be doing is setting the stage for those situations.

Sometimes our behavior is ironic, isn't it? We try to hang on to others, to express love through our caretaker roles. If we are caught caretakers, we become possessive and dependent. Instead of ensuring against loss, we help develop our own and others' dependence, anger and rebelliousness. Then we wonder what happened. In *Why Do I Think I Am Nothing Without a Man?*, Penelope Russianoff repeatedly illustrates with case examples that men *want* women to be self-reliant and secure, able to make decisions and have opinions.[2]

Women's fears about connecting and self-actualization are closely related to our learned role behaviors. As little girls, we may have been taught that we will be fulfilled eventually when we have a man who loves us and children to take care of. We are measured, and we measure ourselves, by our ability to attract and win a man. Our sense of self-worth is closely associated with our success in that area of life.

Reflect briefly on your own focus as you entered the seventh, eighth or ninth grade. Up until that time, you were probably involved principally with school and physical challenges. You could still compete on the playground or the backyard with *all* the kids. Your girlfriends were your most precious friends.

What happened then? You may have been warned about being a tomboy in such disparaging terms that you learned to inhibit physical challenges. Being smart had its scary side effects, too. Women weren't supposed to be scientists, lawyers or mathematicians. Displaying your intelligence could ensure that you would not be invited out, that you would be a wallflower. However, you *could* use your skills to caretake. Did your focus change to attracting boys?

Another message we frequently received as girls was that childbearing is a woman's most important task— that children are a mother's major responsibility. Our children's successes become our own; their failures become our guilt. Then we are accused of living for the kids or being too deeply involved. To top it off, women are expected to be the "heart" of the family, the most vital cog in the wheel. To this end, many women devote their lives to the family, and some suffer bitter disappointment.

The ultimate problem with the traditional role descriptions is that they limit a woman's sense of self to outside sources. Reinforcement is expected from husbands, children and society in general. That's one of the many ways the duties get confused with the attitudes. The duties appear to reflect the attitudes of loving and caring.

The clue to women's dilemma resides in the word *limit*. We are taught caught caretaker roles. We do undervalue ourselves. We are accustomed to subservience. So, consequently, we haven't learned to trust ourselves, to value our abilities, to act with courage. We are afraid of risk. We lack courage, so we do our "duty."

Reconciling Self-Actualization and Connecting

Refer back to the definition of self-actualization earlier in this chapter. As you can see, self-actualization, although described in mostly behavior terms, in fact reflects an attitude or belief about oneself. What we, as women, are really questioning is how we can live for ourselves and also form bonds with others. On the surface, the two components do not appear to be opposing, and actually they aren't. Yet up until now, we have subscribed to a belief system that sharply divides the two.

As women, we have a distinct advantage. We have been taught the importance of connecting, of loving, of listening, of nurturing. We are familiar with the importance of those qualities and the impact they have on the quality of life. Our roles do not have to be confined, unless, of course, we allow the confinement or impose it on ourselves.

Our connecting values are vital to a fulfilled life. What we, as women, are addressing is how to combine our values, our attitudes, and beliefs with meaningful self-expression.

There are challenges for women in the work force, certainly. Perhaps we can influence the corporate world, the working world, to become more oriented toward human values. It's time now to learn new rules for a new game. Up until now, the rules have been written by men; the creativity of women has not been considered, nor even allowed. We can rewrite the rules—not without turmoil, but it can be done. It may, ultimately, be up to women to initiate constructive change.

One analogy I like to use is that while men were learning to play poker, women were learning to play bridge. That is, while men learned that the best hand wins, women learned important rules, innuendoes and subtleties.

We, as women, are capable of new definitions for ourselves. We can choose which qualities are important to us and reject the others. We can learn to discriminate between our attitudes of caretaker and the duties of caretaking. We can enhance our self-definitions by exploring opportunities and options. We can reduce our dependency upon others' approval. We can give up controlling. We do not need to fear loss and rejection.

By the way, the answer I gave to the question "If you don't do your sons' laundry, how do they know you love them?" was, after a moment of thought, "We have fun together."

Notes

1. Mildred Newman and Bernard Berkowitz, with Jean Owen, *How to Be Your Own Best Friend* (New York: Random House, 1971).

2. Penelope Russianoff, *Why Do I Think I Am Nothing Without a Man?* (New York: Bantam Books, 1982).

3

....

Your Message from the Past

"Don't put the catsup bottle on the table." The sentence was the client's answer to my question, "What single message do you remember most from your childhood?"

Cindy, the attractive young woman sitting in my office, had made repeated suicide attempts. When I inquired about the meaning of her answer, she replied that it meant she was supposed to be perfect all the time. Professionally, Cindy was in a demanding job that required her to work with a diversified population of young people and their families in addition to her other managerial responsibilities. There were many environmental influences over which she had no control, and she was working within a limited time frame and budget. You can easily imagine the feelings she had every day, several times a day, about not being able to handle it all—that is, about not being perfect.

Identifying Your Message

What was the message you received in your childhood? It may take some thought to figure it out, or it may be very clear. Try to state it in one sentence if possible, and pay close attention to your interpretation. It may actually have been said repeatedly or it may have been implied through modeling behavior. For example, your parents were hard workers, so the message and expectation was that you should be a hard worker, too. Or the message might have been that angry feelings were never to be expressed; you were forbidden to display angry behavior. Perhaps your family was a family of achievers, so you were expected to achieve, perhaps to excel. If your parents did not have high self-esteem, you were not to feel good about yourself. The messages run the gamut of individual growing-up situations. Understanding the message from your childhood will help you to comprehend your present feelings, thoughts and behaviors.

As you know, understanding your past is one of the most important tools to gain self-awareness, self-acquaintance and self-acceptance. Understanding and accepting are two very different things, although they are frequently confused. Understanding can lead to acceptance when we prohibit ourselves from feeling victimized, holding others responsible for our feelings and behavior. Instead, we assume self-management.

Adopting Coping Behaviors

Let me illustrate the importance of early childhood messages with another example. A young woman, Laura, struggled with the rejecting behaviors and attitudes of her mother. The message she heard over and over again as a child was, "What's *wrong* with you?" She continued to give herself this message. If her husband made a suggestion of something for her to consider, his suggestion, in Laura's mind, was a criticism accompanied by, "What's wrong with you?" He was afraid to say almost anything except the most loving, affectionate words, which she often had difficulty believing.

Of course, this restriction did not lead to open communication. Instead he felt frustrated and angry that his assertions were considered—interpreted, that is—to be criticisms. Laura tried to control the "criticisms" by reacting in an aggressive, attacking manner. Her husband correctly interpreted her reactions as controlling. Since he grew up with controlling parents, his message was that "others are in control," and he responded with his well-practiced way of handling the control—withdrawal and silence, his choices as a child—which led to Laura's magnified fear of criticism, rejection and loss. The communication system between them was clearly dysfunctional.

As illustrated in the above example, each of us learns behaviors to help us cope with the messages from our childhood. Laura learned that the way to manage her frightening feelings of rejection was to behave aggressively. Her husband used withdrawal and silence to handle his fear of being controlled. These behaviors had actually worked as well as possible in the past, but they are inappropriate in the present situation. Keep in mind that the behaviors were helpful at one time, so they are not "bad" or "awful" but simply contrary now to the goals of handling the fears and maintaining peaceful, happy relationships. Predictably, Laura, because she had a difficult time accepting herself, acted out her low self-esteem with other self-destructive behaviors.

Each of us grew up in our individual environment, interacted with our parents or parental figures, felt many feelings and had many experiences. All of this we bring into our present life. Susan, for example, grew up with an alcoholic father and a co-dependent mother who acted like a dependent child. Susan, now in her late forties, understands that sometimes she feels like a frightened child when she is faced with responsibilities. She was the one in charge when she was a child, and, frightened by the responsibility, she ineffectively tried to control her parents. Until she understood her message, "You, little girl, are in charge," she, as an adult, tried to control everyone close to her.

Changing Behaviors

The messages are very potent and will have a pervasive influence on you until you understand them. Your task is to manage your reactions by recognizing and acknowledging the feelings, thinking about your choices and then carrying out your choice of behavior. Your childhood and your message may not have been what you would have liked. You can grieve for that childhood, but you cannot eliminate it. What you can do is accept the reality of and message from your childhood and then use your understanding and acceptance as your management tools.

This may all sound a bit lonely—actually the basic responsibility *is* individual—but we can ask for help. That's connecting. Laura and her husband are helpful to each other now. It's her responsibility to make sure she doesn't interpret his assertions as, "What's wrong with you?" He helps by reminding her that he is not being critical but instead wants open communication. She reminds herself that aggressive behavior is controlling behavior. He prevents himself from withdrawing and she helps by reminding him that she is not trying to control him. This type of change occurs when you treat yourself and others with trust and respect, when you practice self-management skills and when you accord self- and mutual reinforcement.

In Cindy's case, her primary task was to understand and accept that her "perfect" message is impossible to achieve. Perfection, like beauty, is in the eye of the beholder, not an absolute measurement. She can ask others for support and encouragement. Susan can remind herself that the others in her life are not dependent parents. Those others can help by kindly refusing to cooperate with any control she might try to exert.

You may be asking now if all the messages are negative or painful. Unfortunately, many are because many of us have had a lot of pain in our lives. Seemingly at the other end of the spectrum is Peter, who reported that every day of his life he was told, "I love you" at least once, but usually several times. He came to my office because his wife wasn't loving enough, at least as far as he was concerned, and he found himself demanding love. His wife, Sara, on the other hand, had had a series of poor relationships that verified her message from her mother that, "all men are no good and not to be trusted."

In the process of their work, they discovered that they had an agenda in their marriage that had been under cover. Peter wanted to prove to Sara that men really are lovable and trustworthy. Sara steadfastly resisted in order to eventually discourage him and prove to herself once again that men are no good and not to be trusted. This was one of the systems in their relationship. There is more about systems in Chapter 11.

Understanding and Accepting Your Message

What is your message from the past? Chances are that you learned it quite well and it remains an important influential factor in your life. By understanding your message, you can use it to gain self-acquaintance and self-management. By accepting your message you can give yourself the freedom from the bondage of blaming others. You will be able to reinforce your high self-worth.

One of my favorite reminder phrases is, "Life is what happens to me in spite of what I've planned." You cannot control life, but you can manage by being flexible and self-aware and by trusting yourself.

4

. . . .

Thoughts, Behavior and Feelings:

Especially Anger

When you were growing up, how did you learn about feelings? Did you learn to discriminate your feelings from your thoughts? Your feelings from your behavior? What are the differences? How often do you say, "I feel" when you really mean, "I think?" Perhaps *feel* sounds a little softer than *think*, or it's just a way of talking, or it doesn't seem to matter which word you choose.

The truth is that we seldom are taught to make a distinction between thoughts and feelings. Sometimes we learn to distinguish thoughts and feelings from behaviors. That's a little easier. But we don't always know the difference. Take anger, for example. *Anger* is often described as a feeling that is violent and out of control: temper, a clutch in the stomach, harsh words, impulsive action followed by regret. Anger is almost never described as an acceptable feeling, but analyzed instead in behavioral terms.

Learning about Thoughts, Behavior and Feelings

Did you learn about the importance of feelings? Probably not as easily as you learned about the importance of thinking. Thinking is reinforced as being more practical and useful than feeling, and we are taught that idea many ways in school. Originally, it was through reading, writing and arithmetic. Today we can add computer science, aerodynamics and environmental conservation. We are encouraged to learn skills and trades, to achieve and to excel. Skills and achievements are important, of course. They contribute to our experiencing high self-worth and supporting ourselves financially.

As children, we were also taught to behave in certain specified ways, to be mannerly and obedient. As little girls we were often rewarded for being quiet and agreeable. We might have received praise for our behavior, but were taught at the same time that we shouldn't feel prideful.

A few courses in school, such as psychology, sociology, health and family life, touch on feelings. But, generally, learning to understand and accept our feelings is neglected in the formal educational process.

We are not taught that feeling and thinking and behavior are closely connected yet separate. Our feelings provide the motivation for our thinking, which in turn activates the behavior. To add to the confusion, without an awareness of the separation of feelings and thinking and behavior, we sometimes operate on automatic pilot, unaware of what feelings are motivating us. We run the risk of screening out one-third of ourselves. The wheel, as first seen in Chapter 2, looks like this:

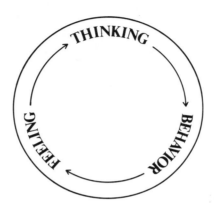

Behavior or an event triggers the feelings that motivate the thinking. We use the behavior to respond to the feelings and thinking. The behavior may trigger another go-around. And so it goes, over and over. Sometimes we may also go around the circle with the pattern:

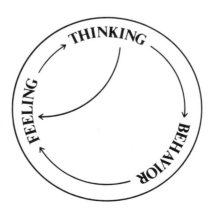

We may have many feelings and thoughts before we initiate behavior(s). This illustrates a greater complexity, but it does not invalidate the original interaction. Our best bet, then, is to acquaint ourselves with the whole system as well as we can.

Women are very often "feelings" people. Although feelings are a valuable asset, we have to remember that in our society people are judged by their *thoughts* and *behavior*. It would be a serious mistake to assume that feelings are of more consequence than thoughts and behavior. The goal is to understand and to value, and at the same time to separate yet integrate, the three important components of ourselves: thoughts, behavior and feelings.

Classifying Feelings

I'm not going to ask you to list feelings; the number would undoubtedly be almost endless. But it will be helpful for our exploration to classify all feelings into four categories: sad, mad, glad and scared,[1] or grief, anger, love and fear.

As a child, you probably learned that some feelings are positive or good, and therefore acceptable, and that other feelings are negative or bad, and therefore unacceptable. You probably also determined that if you had a positive or good feeling, you were good; if you had a negative or bad feeling, you were bad. Consider that idea for a minute.

It's easy to understand how you might have learned that message. Children don't express feelings verbally; they act them out. They quickly comprehend that when they act in certain ways, they are rewarded or punished. Children don't learn to discriminate between their feelings and behavior. The way they behave seems to be the way they feel or vice versa.

Are you beginning to comprehend how people are sometimes described as behaving childishly? They go from feelings to behavior without thinking. Their wheel looks like this:

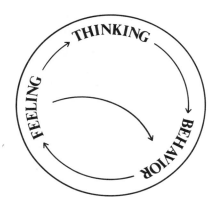

They haven't learned how to separate their feelings, their thoughts and their behavior, or to value feeling and thinking and behaving. You can begin to learn the distinction. Let's start with an examination of self-management.

Self-Management

Believing that you are capable of self-management is an extremely important attitude for effective living. In the previous chapters, we've explored how women have been taught to rely upon others' approval and how the messages from the past can impact us. By complying with the caught caretaker role, women learn implied dependency. Self-management will help women combine connecting and self-actualization.

Often we use the word *control.* "Control yourself" is a message others give us. But it's also one we frequently give ourselves. What we're talking about, of course, is controlling our behavior, and maybe our feelings, although in the confusion they are practically indistinguishable.

The word *control* can be limiting. The dictionary definition includes the words *authority, dominate* and *restrain.* We very often put the lid on ourselves when we "control ourselves." Controlling others implies an autocratic, overbearing power.

Management, however, signifies a continuum of *response* and *initiative,* words that suggest success in doing or accomplishing. By thinking of self-management as an acquired skill, you can recognize that by assuming self-management and believing that you are capable of it, you are acknowledging your responsibility for and to yourself in all varieties of circumstances.

When you reinforce your high self-worth with self-management skills, you enable yourself to believe that you can handle whatever comes your way, that you can take charge of your own life, set goals and pursue them. To apply self-management, it is important to understand feeling, thinking and behaving.

But many women inhibit self-management. Despite the overwhelming logic for self-management, they still cling to learned dependency behaviors. They continue waiting to be rescued—waiting for someone else to make decisions and tell them how to lead their lives.

Why? Why do women try to fit themselves into predescribed definition boxes to avoid self-management?

Is it guilt? When the caretaker role is acted out by sacrifice and self-denial and the expected results don't materialize, the caught caretaker will feel guilty, believing she didn't caretake enough or do it right.

But guilt does nothing to motivate self-responsibility, although it *looks* like a woman is being self-responsible by feeling guilty, doesn't it? What she did, the way she defined and confined herself didn't work. Maybe she bought into sex role stereotypes; maybe she inhibited her professional achievement; maybe she learned to avoid decision making.

Could it be shame? Shame is closely related to guilt. A woman may feel ashamed that she didn't succeed in the way she should have. Others can see her "failures," her "mistakes." In addition, if she's done something she *shouldn't* have, in violation of her shoulds, her shame is magnified.

For many women shame is reinforced by comparing themselves unfavorably to other women. Some of the currently popular literature defines the new way a woman should be. But often she doesn't believe herself to be capable of meeting all the new definitions, all the while telling herself that she should have changed long before now. Sometimes a woman's response is wanting to hide out in her caught caretaker role, avoiding self-management. The irony is that for her to feel guilt and shame is socially acceptable.

What about fear? We've learned very well to underestimate our abilities, sometimes in spite of outstanding evidence of competence. We may believe that if we learn to take care of ourselves no one will take care of us. We continue to describe ourselves by what we do instead of who we are. We may be afraid to risk a new option or a new definition. There may be a fear of not connecting or of losing others important to us.

Look closely at all your fears. How do you describe them? The fear of success? Commitment? Risk? Failure? Intimacy? Whatever your fears may be, the common denominator is the *fear of loss*. Are you controlled by your fear of loss? Do you inhibit your self-management because of guilt, shame and the fear of loss? Look at the loss factor in guilt and shame.

To inhibit your self-management is a violation of your high self-esteem. And what is the result of that violation? *Anger.*

Anger

Feeling guilty gets tiresome. Admittedly, some women live a lifetime feeling guilty, but guilt can mask anger. Shame can mask anger. At the root of the anger is this: What we expect for ourselves—perhaps what our mothers taught us to expect—doesn't fit our reality. Self-sacrifice turned out to be exactly that. No one, or very few, appeared to appreciate the martyrdom. The promised rewards didn't materialize.

Children leave home and they don't call very often. Lovers stray when they lose interest; they find someone who is really "with it." Our employers don't appreciate our efforts. Husbands want divorces; life is passing them, and you, by. Grandchildren are being raised differently from the way you did it. You aren't trained to be on your own. You're guilty and ashamed and fearful and angry.

But anger, you've learned, is not okay. In order to understand, let's look closely at anger and the ways the feeling is misunderstood, disguised and feared.

Let's go back to sad, mad, glad and scared, and also to good and bad feelings. Sad and scared feelings are generally not labeled "good" or "bad." They are somewhat neutral, although they may be quite painful. They include feelings of grief, sorrow, regret, fear, shame and guilt. There are probably others you could name.

Glad feelings are the good feelings. Love always tops the list, followed by joy, compassion, empathy, sympathy, tenderness and sexiness. Mad is bad. Mad includes anger, jealousy, envy, rivalry, hatred and criticism. Add any of your own bad feelings.

For little girls, it's okay to be sad, glad or scared. But not mad. Especially not angry. Be a caught caretaker, to the maximum, but for heaven's sake, don't get mad. That's not feminine.

If we're angry, we aren't caretaking. The whole family will be upset. If we're angry, we aren't feminine. If we're angry, we're aggressive, pushy or bitchy. If we're angry, we're out of control and certainly not behaving reasonably. If we're angry, we're not mature. If we're angry, we "just don't understand." Do you see how angry feelings and angry behavior get so mixed up? Anger is not an allowable feeling for women to have. If that seems like an overstatement, question yourself and other women.

In our learned caught caretaker role, we also do not acknowledge that we have opinions and rights. Have you ever thought about your personal rights? Most women have not, so they allow a lot of violations. If you haven't any personal rights, how can they be breached? How can you possibly be angry?

We have a well-learned denial of self—that is, until something goes awry in our world. Then how do we feel? Guilty! Guilty, shamed and fearful. Guilt and shame keep the lid on anger because women have confused the feeling of anger and angry behavior. So what do we do with the anger, the feeling? Well, we are allowed to be hurt, disappointed, frustrated, upset, annoyed, disgusted or irritated—but *not* angry. We devise a lot of alias feelings in an attempt to disguise our real anger. How is it that we get all those alias feelings mixed up with anger? Let's start with hurt.

Anger Aliases

Is it more acceptable to be hurt than to be angry? What is hurt? Hurt implies a passivity. Someone has done something to us. We are helpless in the face of another's expressions, words or actions. We say, "You hurt my feelings." Can you comprehend the passivity in that statement? The speaker might as well also be saying, "You need to do something about what you did. How I feel is your responsibility."

Yet, there is such a thing as hurt. It's generally thought of as the feeling one has when trust, confidence or intimacy is breached by someone who is especially close to us. Anger, however, is *the feeling response to the violation, abuse or disregard of one's personal principles, values, property and self.* Consider the definition and you can easily understand that when you violate your high self-esteem through guilt, shame and fear, you will feel angry.

There are important differences between anger and hurt, as well as between anger and disappointment. We're disappointed when an expectation isn't met—again, passivity. Is there anger in disappointment?

What is frustration? Frustration can lead to anger. We may even *be* angry, but we say we're frustrated; passivity enters. Anger is too active a response.

Upset, annoyance, irritation and disgust have been called levels of anger and there is truth to the description. Being annoyed is different from being disgusted, which may be milder than feeling intensely angry. The point is to notice whether you use the substitute words when you really mean, "I'm angry." Sometimes women will talk of resentment instead of anger. It's an ineffective word substitution because resentment is old anger that has been stored up, collected and not expressed.

Another disguise for anger is anxiety. We're so fearful that an expression of anger will cost us relationships, jobs or control that we substitute anxiety for anger. Think about the times you've experienced fear. You've probably felt anxious, nervous and uptight as well.

Yet another disguise is depression. A depressed woman is more socially acceptable than an angry one. Hopelessness (no hope for things to be better, your relatives to change, your job to improve, etc.) combines with guilt and shame to produce depression. Depression can become very serious, producing multiple physical and emotional effects. Then we get treated for being depressed instead of angry.

Another choice is to become chronically tired instead of acknowledging the anger. If you've ever allowed yourself to honestly feel anger, you can imagine how much energy is used to suppress it, and if you combine the suppression with anxiety, no wonder you're tired. You want to sleep all the time. Sometimes we give ourselves illnesses such as obesity, anorexia, addiction, insomnia, frequent headaches and ulcers. Then we're sick instead of angry.

Why Is Anger a No-No?

So why aren't women supposed to be angry? Why don't women allow themselves to feel angry? Why is anger so hard to handle?

To start with, if you were taught that anger is a bad feeling, then you didn't want it. Chances are, your logic was something on the order of, "If I feel anger, a bad feeling, then I'm bad." Not wanting to feel bad about yourself, you might have tried to suppress your anger.

Then, your parents may have scolded you. They probably did not discriminate between your behavior and your anger. Throwing a tantrum in the grocery store is angry *behavior*. For parents, it's also embarrassing, irritating and unacceptable. In many ways it's not desirable to be an angry person. We're probably all in agreement that angry people often act out their anger by being blaming, guilt-inducing, unfriendly, controlling and just plain unpleasant. Who wants that?

We may also have been taught that it's not polite to express feelings of "mad," although it's okay to be sad, glad or scared. Finally, religious beliefs may enter into the denial of anger: To be angry is to sin. We're instructed instead to turn the other cheek.

What kind of verbal messages about anger did you hear as a child? Perhaps something similar to:

"Nice little girls don't get angry."
"If you're angry, I won't love you."
"If you're angry, you won't be liked."
"If you're angry, I'll know you don't love me."
"Go to your room until you can behave."
"Big girls don't get angry."

But probably the most prevalent message against anger comes to women as they learn their role of caught caretaker. How can we caretake and also be angry? Is anger contrary to caretaking? Is anger destructive to connecting? Does anger inhibit self-actualization?

Anger is a universal feeling. Everyone experiences anger. Remember, it's the feeling response to a violation.

It's not the feeling of anger that is destructive. What can be destructive is angry behavior.

Angry Behaviors

Unloading, dumping, blaming, finger-pointing behavior is, indeed, very destructive. In my private practice, couples will occasionally come for marriage counseling after years of destructive angry behavior. Frequently, there is little to do. Angry feelings have not been appropriately addressed for so long that angry behavior has destroyed the marriage.

What are some of the behaviors we use to conceal anger?

One is gossiping. Talking about another to someone else may very well be an expression of anger that we don't allow ourselves to confront directly. "I don't really want to say anything bad, but. . . ." With this kind of indirect behavior, we are also concealing our fear that we couldn't handle the response of the person at whom we're angry. So we try to avoid the confrontation. We are fearful about what might happen.

We're blunt. We say we're only being honest, "telling you this for your own good." Then we let the other person have our "opinions" directly and sometimes cruelly. The whole interaction resembles a wolf in sheep's clothing.

We use sarcasm. Sarcasm is usually considered to be acceptable behavior because it sounds funny. It has even reached new heights with people-roast dinners. Yet sarcasm can hide a lot of anger or jealousy or envy and criticism. Sarcasm's close relative, teasing, operates in the same ways.

We complain. Have you ever watched an old-fashioned tea kettle boil? The lid may rise and fall until the steam is released. Women do the same thing. They "tea-kettle," complaining to someone else until the steam (anger) is reduced. Or they complain more directly: "If only you...," "You need to...," "Everyone else is going." Complaining and whining and nagging are a lot alike. They're indirect and dishonest because they obscure the real feelings and thoughts we have.

If others feel angry when we tea kettle, whine or nag, we, by avoiding self-management, believe that's their responsibility. If they had done what they were supposed to do, or acted the way they should have, we wouldn't have had to tell them.

We cry. Many women release the physical components of anger by crying. Then they describe themselves as ashamed, out of control and childish. If you do cry and you can't identify the reason very quickly, check to see if you are really angry about something. Use your crying as an important clue.

We try to get someone else to be the angry person for us. That way, we're not responsible. We may even marry an angry person. Then we pay a big price.

If we allow ourselves to be aware of our angry feelings, how do we sometimes behave so that we distort a direct, honest and sincere expression? One way is to displace the anger onto someone other than the appropriate person. We use the familiar pecking order, from superior to inferior. We're angry about something that occurred in another setting; then we pick on a friend or a family member. Another way is to delay expressing ourselves, reasoning that it's not an appropriate time or place. That could actually be helpful if you address your feeling later. Instead, women often decide later that "it isn't worth making problems now" or "it wasn't important," and do nothing.

We clam up and don't say anything. We believe that to be angry is to not love. We deep-freeze our anger so that we tell ourselves we never get angry. It may seem that way, too, because when anger has been hidden for a long time we don't recognize it. We water down the anger by rationalizing or justifying, saying things like, "Maybe I overreacted," "She didn't really mean anything by her remark," "That's just the way he is," "It's really my fault." Rationalizing and justifying are big traps for women. Watch for them in your own behavior. They are very different from explaining. Explaining is based on a desire to be understood. Rationalizing and justifying are based on a desire to be excused.

We're supposed to be in control of ourselves. We believe that feeling angry is being out of control. Indeed, sometimes angry *behavior* is evidence of being out of control. We escalate the risk of being out of control when we distort or disguise angry feelings. We allow small angers to build into gigantic angers and then we behave by exploding and feeling shame about the explosion; everyone around us retreats. We assume it's our fault; then we feel guilty and risk repeating the entire scenario.

There are two extremely common angry behaviors that merit being singled out. One is passive-aggressive behavior. Let me give you an example, then see if you fall into this behavior sometimes.

My husband, on his way out of the house in the morning, asks me to do a few errands for him: mail a package, pick up the dry cleaning and call the dentist. I'm on the way out too. The kids have gone off on the bus and I have to leave so I'll be on time at my job. I agree to do the errands. After all, I get off at 4:30, and I have my lunch hour; but my principal motivation for agreeing is that "good wives" do these sorts of things (my caught caretaker).

So I do the errands. When I finally arrive home, the kids are there, with dirty lunchboxes sitting in the kitchen. They haven't started their homework or piano practice. Of course, it's up to me to see that they do those things. My caught caretaker assumes responsibility for their success, instead of teaching them self-management. Supper is still to be prepared, and there is laundry to do.

So what do I prepare? Canned chicken noodle soup. Oh yes, I know they all hate it, especially my husband. But darn it all, they just *load* things onto me and I don't have time to fix a decent meal. If they're mad about supper it's *their* fault!

That's an example of passive-aggressive behavior, but a very mild one. The behavior is usually much more complicated.

The second angry behavior is similar because it also involves passivity. Passive-resistant behavior is marked by the inhibition of honest, sincere and direct expressions of feelings and thoughts. People who use it do not actively express opposition, but they block something from happening by resisting action without offering constructive alternatives.

When passive-resistance is used to hide anger, the resistant (and angry) person will focus on problems with another's plans, refuse to help, or agree to help but not get around to it. Another's frustration is the goal. When solutions are suggested, the passive-resistant person ignores them. She or he may indulge in help-rejecting complaining.

In addition, passive-resistant people will suppress enjoyment or enthusiasm, and instead cast a wet blanket of boredom, patronizing tolerance or martyred endurance on another's excitement, dreams or activities. While they don't necessarily refuse to participate, they withhold the energy of full commitment. They behaviorally act out their anger in a quietly subversive manner.

What women have learned to do well by suppressing anger is to suppress assertion. They are passive until the proverbial straw that broke the camel's back, and then they feel justifiably angry.

They are desperately trying to get others to feel responsible for them. They feel dependent. They feel a need to be loved. They are well-schooled caught caretakers. But their learned dependency leads to passivity, helplessness and consequent anger, which they frequently express by choosing destructive behavior.

What are the options? What can women do to allow themselves to experience all the feelings? Including anger.

First, familiarize yourself with the differences between feelings, thoughts and behavior. If you've not allowed the so-called bad feelings, remind yourself that feelings are feelings only. They are not good or bad, negative or positive. Instead, judge the behavior that you choose to express the feelings.

Then look at how you choose the behavior. You use thinking, your intelligence and your knowledge. Pay close attention to how you are interpreting events in your life. You may want to seek out professional help for this exploration in order to increase objectivity. Read to expand your awareness. Question opinions and predescribed definitions. Think about how you learned your roles. Are the definitions good for you now?

Believe in yourself. Use your high self-esteem to

help yourself build self-management skills. If you find yourself resistant, remind yourself that you have old, well-learned dependencies. Denial of oneself necessarily means other-directedness.

If you have special difficulty with anger, examine fully all the disguises and cover-ups described earlier. See if they fit you.

Ask yourself how anger was expressed in your family. Did open display of angry behavior lead to your denying your feeling? Or was concealment your model, perhaps because anger was considered a sin?

There's no debate that certain angry behaviors are difficult to handle for both the giver and the receiver. We try to inhibit angry behavior because we, in the position of either giver or receiver, don't know that there are options for expressing our anger other than some form of aggressiveness. We allow ourselves to be frightened; we say we don't like confrontations. But by being aware of our feelings and choosing our behavior— using self-management skills—we can select from many ideas about how to handle anger.

Each of us has our own self-acceptable behavior choices. When you allow yourself the recognition that you do indeed sometimes experience anger, you may judge yourself to be an angry person. While that's possible, it's not too probable. It is probable that you are simply allowing yourself a broader recognition of *all* your feelings. It's important that as you allow yourself to recognize your angry feelings, you also have some idea of how to handle them.

Constructive Angry Behavior

The most outstanding example of constructive angry behavior was told by a young woman in one of my groups. As I was explaining the difference between the feeling of anger and angry behavior, I could see Martha's face noticeably change, her eyes light up and a smile start. "I finally understand what I've done!" she exclaimed. She has been told all her life that she shouldn't try this, she better not do that, the task would be too difficult. She related how really angry she felt. Her choice of behavior to handle her anger was to accomplish the goals she set for herself. Today Martha is quite successful in a complicated, detail-vital profession. Her choice of behavior to handle her anger is to succeed and to continue to succeed. Martha has cerebral palsy.

Another choice is to remind yourself that assertive expressions of anger actually help build relationships. Challenge any early beliefs you might have that suppressing anger will build relationships and denying anger is caretaking. Reflect on the examples of disguises and alternate behaviors that are destructive.

When we feel angry toward someone we care about, we display confidence in them and ourselves when we are able to say directly and simply, "I feel angry because . . ." Restricting aggressive behavior will lend credence to your assertion. The other person is more likely to listen.

If you start out your declaration of anger with an accusation ("You. . . "), the other person will automatically become defensive. It's much more likely that an argument will follow and all your fears will appear to be justified. If you have stated your assertion starting with "I. . . ," listen carefully to the reply. Do not allow your feeling of anger to screen out whatever the other person is saying; your goal is a discussion, not an argument.

Avoid trying to establish right or wrong, fair or unfair, just or unjust. I'll discuss this point more fully in Chapter 11.

I want to emphasize clearly that I am not advocating hanging onto anger, being an angry person, or continually interpreting life events so that you feel anger. My emphasis is quite the opposite. Allow yourself *all* your feelings. When you feel angry, decide how to handle that feeling as quickly as possible. Determine your choice of action and then don't allow yourself to cling to anger. That's resentment and resentment will cause emotional distress and serious illnesses.

Focus on positiveness in your life. A direct, sincere and honest expression of anger, or any of the associated uncomfortable feelings, can be as positive as expressions of love, joy, compassion, empathy or tenderness—the comfortable feelings. I believe that recognizing and allowing the uncomfortable feelings increases our capacity for enjoying the comfortable ones.

New Behaviors for New Lives

Please, remember: The purpose of this book is to encourage you to formulate your own answers, to explore, examine, retain, discard and decide. Be kind to yourself as you decide. We have developed behavior patterns because they have worked. We can understand that we sometimes continue these patterns into our present life settings. It isn't that we're doing things wrong that once seemed right. What is important is to learn new behaviors that fit into our ever-changing present reality.

Positive growth means allowing yourself to make decisions while remembering that most decisions are themselves temporary. Your life can be reorganized according to new scripts, new ideas and your creativity.

However, don't allow yourself to forever keep your life "in committee," fearful of loss. We keep our lives in committee when we talk and don't act, when we are constantly researching without risking. Sometimes what seems to be a "gut" feeling is actually a fear that new behaviors will lead to loss. Decide what you would like to keep and what you want to change.

One thing is certain: Change is difficult. We tend to cling desperately to old ways. Feelings stop change. We act almost as if we're on automatic pilot. If you do decide that some changes are appropriate, here is a five-step formula to follow. This sequence will apply to any changes you wish to make as you develop your awarenesses.

1. *Gain intellectual understanding.* Allow yourself to be open to options, new ideas and other opinions. Flexibility is based on high self-esteem; rigidity is cemented in fear. Choose your opinions carefully so that they are in accord with your values, principles and religious beliefs. It does no good to try to deny aspects of your heritage that are important to you.

2. *Choose behavior.* Be creative. Don't allow yourself to be confined by other people's formulas. Sometimes our reality seems to be revolving so quickly, *nothing* predescribed appears to be appropriate. Pick and choose. Since changing is a long-term thing, you can afford to give yourself the luxury of contemplation. But don't allow yourself to remain in committee. Use your high self-esteem to encourage risks and trials.

3. *Confront the old fear.* This is the hard part. What stops us from change is our fear of loss. Even when we contemplate a change from our former behavior we encounter the old fearfulness. We tell ourselves that it just

doesn't seem right, or we scare ourselves by asking, "What if...?" Remember that fear comes from the past. Remind yourself that you are choosing to stay in the present and you have decided to make a change. Your decision is based on good evidence. You're willing to risk because you're feeling strong and you want to reinforce your decision to enjoy high self-worth.

4. *Effect the behavior.* Use your self-management skills. Do not allow yourself to succumb to your fear. For example, if you have decided to be assertive about your anger, you will probably have to force yourself the first time you say, "I feel angry because...."

5. *Reinforce yourself.* Your feelings of pride and accomplishment are your most valuable rewards. These feelings say, "I did it and I'm glad!" You may find it necessary to reinforce yourself over and over. That's the way you will change your feelings about your new behavior. Sometimes outside reinforcement is sparse or nonexistent, or remarks are critical. Sometimes when we want to change, others don't want us to. So they play the old game harder. They may want you to be like you were before because they haven't recognized or realized the appropriateness of your behavior changes. They may be fearful or they may interpret your new behavior as threatening, challenging or detrimental to their well-being.

We set our own parameters of experience. We constrain our own curiosity. We allow ourselves to feel low self-esteem and our fear is magnified. We try to fit ourselves into rigid little boxes of how to live our lives. We do those things to ourselves. Even though we have understandings of how and why, we allow ourselves to assign responsibility to society, our jobs or our families.

It takes courage to change. We limit ourselves to old options because we're afraid of loss. We're afraid to differ too much from one another. We're apprehensive about trying new behaviors and taking risks. We don't want to be criticized or condemned or thought of as difficult. We're frightened of losing our image or maybe of having an image that stands out. We buy into the way it *should* be. We're just plain afraid of being wrong.

Use self-management skills to reinforce your high self-worth. Creativity and new options are how you think about things and how you put ideas together in new ways. Use old ideas and bring them into the present, but remodel them if you decide it's necessary. Allow *all* your feelings and examine your thoughts and your interpretations. Then make decisions about your behavior.

Notes

1. John W. Travis and Regina Sara Ryan, *The Wellness Workbook* (Berkeley, Calif.: Ten Speed Press, 1981), p. 127.

5

Should Is a Dirty Word

Some years ago in my private practice, Kathy came to see me because she suffered severe migraine headaches. She had heard that biofeedback could be helpful.[1]

I began to work with Kathy, first teaching her relaxation techniques and temperature control, and assisting her practice with the biofeedback instruments. After a few visits, she was feeling comfortable with me and she began to talk about her life. I encouraged her to talk, because the process of biofeedback alone is not sufficient to achieve long-term management of migraine headaches.

The more I listened to Kathy, the more aware I became that what she was saying was peppered with the word *should*. "My husband should not be so sullen and mean." (He actually was verbally and physically abusive.) "My son should make better grades." (He was quitting school.) "My daughter should help more at home." (Kathy often didn't know what her daughter was doing.) "I should be able to go to college for the training I require."(That seemed to be an impossibility.) "I should be an efficient real-estate broker." (She was a real-estate office clerk.)

You can see that Kathy's life was not the way she thought it should be. Her real life was quite opposite to her shoulds. She allowed herself to obscure that fact. Until she realized how she was disguising her life, she prevented any change. In some ways, Kathy's shoulds almost sounded hopeful, as if the day after tomorrow life would be better, the way it *should* be. In reality, however, she kept herself victimized by her shoulds.

The Should Victim

Kathy made herself a victim by concentrating on how her life should be instead of how her life actually was. She prevented her own exploration and expansion. Her shoulds were excuses for the way life was for her and she didn't take the risks to change her reality. She was too fearful. Kathy viewed herself as helpless and powerless to control her life. She failed to recognize her abilities to develop personal power. This led to a bottling-up of her anger and low self-esteem, and eventually to their disguise as debilitating migraine headaches. Also, Kathy didn't realize that she was continually criticizing herself and others.

How is *should* critical? When someone (you, he, she, the family, the next-door neighbor, your friend, the postal clerk, etc.) *should*, that means that person *isn't*. Kathy viewed her world and herself critically, with distrust and doubt and with little or no hope.

For a minute, try to put yourself into Kathy's shoes. Think about how often you say *should, need to, ought to, have to* or *must*. The words are interchangeable. Make up a message to yourself about something you should be doing, but aren't. As you say your sentence, what feeling do you have? Often the feeling is guilt. When you tell yourself you should, but actually you're not, you'll probably experience some shame, guilt and non-self-acceptance. *You* contribute to your own feelings of low self-esteem. It's extremely important that you accept responsibility for the nonacceptance. Don't permit yourself to try to blame the world, your family, your employer, your spouse, your lover or your parents because they aren't the way they should be. When you give up blaming, you assume self-management.

When you give up guilt, you can start self-actualizing and you can combine it with connecting. Why? Because guilt, the token feeling, very frequently disguises anger, as we saw in Chapter 4. Guilt and anger inhibit both connecting and self-actualization.

When you haven't done what you should, you feel guilty. When you feel guilty long enough, you begin to feel uncomfortable (maybe impatient, anxious, edgy, moody). Since feeling uncomfortable is not acceptable for very long, you return to leading your life the way you want. Without examination of your life-style, you can repeat the entire routine.

Nothing has changed and possibly you begin to feel anger in addition to guilt. That's because you are trying to lead your life the way you should instead of the way you want. You feel hurt, frustrated, upset, disappointed, disgusted or irritated, your alias feelings for anger. But feeling angry may not be okay either, because you are self-denying. Caught caretakers are not supposed to feel angry. So, instead, you feel guilty.

Sometimes it seems that the only allowable feelings for women are *love* (expressed in caught caretaking), *grief* (such as when a death occurs), *fear* (that resides in our learned powerlessness) and *guilt* (we should, but we don't).

After a number of sessions Kathy began to understand how she was limiting her potential through all the shoulds she imposed on herself. We made a little sign— "*Should* is a dirty word"—and she began to work to remove herself from the victim position.

Shoulds vs. Wants

Perhaps the following written and thought-promoting exercise will help you begin to understand how you may be conducting your life according to some shoulds.

Divide a piece of paper in half by drawing or folding a line down the center. Head one side *Should* and the other side *Want*. On the should side, list all the things you should be doing, all the ways you should be thinking or feeling. On the want side, list all the things you want to do, all the ways you want to be.

Give yourself plenty of time to make your lists. Then ask yourself these questions.

1. *How many of the shoulds are role-defined?* For help, refer to Chapter 2 and the roles you've described for yourself. Then determine whether any of your shoulds are dictated by your perceived role descriptions.

2. *Are your shoulds supporting to your self-definition?* Do they fit in with the ways you've defined yourself? Pay attention to determine whether your shoulds are the ways you *think you should be instead of the ways you actually*

are. If you do use your shoulds in an attempt to support your self-definition, you turn them into right or the right way. Then you present yourself as "having all the answers," as rigid and self-righteous. This is contrary to connecting, because you are unaccepting of others.

3. *Where did you learn your should messages?* Parents? Religion? Employers? Teachers? Husband? Friends? The feminist movement? Advertising? Magazine articles? Peer pressure? Your mother-in-law?

It becomes easily apparent that many of the messages may have originally come from outside yourself. Now you can understand how you might have learned to attach blame. If you believe that your shoulds still come from outside you, in messages from your past or from peers or others, you will inhibit your ability to gain personal power through self-management and self-responsibility. Nothing is gained by telling yourself you would be okay if only someone else would change, if only someone else would do what he or she should do. *It's vital to understand that your present shoulds are self-imposed.*

4. *Have you ever evaluated your shoulds?* Have you given thought to their relevance to you now? Do they fit the realities of your life? In other words, are they meaningful to you now or are they from your past?

By now, you may also be asking whether shoulds are ever any good for you. Look at them carefully again. What do you see in terms of values, principles and structure? There you have your answer. Your shoulds can provide guidelines for how you choose to lead your life, but when you lead your life contrary to the *important, self-determined* shoulds, you run the risk of feeling guilt and/or shame. The difference between retaining guilt and shame and living a free life lies in determining your most important life values, principles and definitions and then leading your life in such ways that you do not violate them.

5. *Are any of the shoulds interchangeable with the wants?* If you are leading your life in ways that are meaningful for you, you will discover that most, perhaps all, of the items are interchangeable. Your want list might include personal goals. Determine how they can be achieved. Sometimes shoulds help achieve wants or goals. They fit into a larger framework. If you want to be a lawyer, you will need to go to law school. You will have to study diligently.

As you can see now, your careful evaluation of your should list is vital to leading your life in the manner that you have determined is best for you. Often we are fearful that if we accept an old message, we will compromise ourselves by accepting parental values, religious doctrines or other people's shoulds. The truth, however, is that when you determine which of the values, past messages and definitions are relevant for you now and which you choose to discard, you are developing a high level of maturity and self-management skills. Then you will have no trouble bringing your two lists together.

Unexamined Shoulds

Without your examination and determination, you will run risks for yourself. Unexamined shoulds can keep you in difficult or impossible situations. For example, a nurse is asked to do double duty. She may determine it's a reasonable request, but she's tired and has other activities planned for the evening. Her caught caretaker role, however, is very well learned. She defines herself as responsible, helpful, compassionate, capable and caring. If she doesn't thoughtfully determine what is important for herself, she may agree to the overtime and additional duties, setting herself up for extreme fatigue, irritability, blaming and anger. However, she *should* do the extra work. See how it can work?

Sometimes we use our shoulds so we can describe ourselves as perfectionists. But no matter how hard we try or how much effort we give to achieving perfection in ourselves or others, we never achieve our goal. Of course not—perfection is beyond reach. We can do our best, we can try our hardest and we can describe the results as perfect. But are they ever perfect? What is perfect anyway?

By describing ourselves as perfectionists, we set unreasonably high standards for ourselves, often leading to an additional problem: procrastination. When we procrastinate, we berate ourselves for being lazy, for lacking foresight and self-discipline. What are we hiding by procrastinating? Low self-esteem and a fear of loss. By waiting until the last minute, we can rationalize that the results weren't really a true test of our abilities.

Then we tell ourselves we should have started earlier; we should have done a better job; we would have been more satisfied with the results, but we're perfectionists. We reinforce our low self-esteem.

Unexamined shoulds are obviously limiting. You can determine for yourself how you lead your life now and how you *want* to lead your life. By accepting your vital and important life values, you can give up guilt and shame and be self-accepting.

Others' Shoulds

Sometimes you may find yourself being challenged by someone else's shoulds or by societal role definitions. There's no question about it, the challenge is difficult.

Others' shoulds are *their* way of life. Whether or not they examine those shoulds is their business. But when others try to impose their shoulds on us, trouble can result. Often others may be trying to control us because of their own insecurity. They want us to live our lives the same way they lead theirs so they will feel reinforced for their way. They may determine that we are too self-willed and be frightened that we will reject them. They may try to hold a tighter rein. Horses bolt when a rein is tightened; you may feel like doing the same thing.

But you have an option. When you feel secure in your own self-definition, in the values, principles and rules you have for yourself, when your goals are your own and when your tasks are the ones you choose, then you will be conducting yourself with self-management skills, you will assume self-responsibility, and you will enjoy your high self-worth.

Caught Caretaker Shoulds

The big trap is the caught caretaker. The caught caretaker role is loaded with shoulds—predescribed, predefined, premodeled. *If we continue to have our connecting values confused with the caretaker duties, we will inhibit self-actualization.*

Once again, it's necessary to examine for yourself, in depth, the interconnections of feelings, thoughts and behavior. It will be important for you to challenge behavioral shoulds that are rigidly role-defined. They could limit self-management and self-expression.

Fear of Change

As you challenge behavioral shoulds, you will encounter the feelings—usually guilt and fear—that keep you stuck. But if you've determined that you will effect your own self-definition based on your examination of how you view yourself, that you will acknowledge your responsibility for yourself and that you will assume self-management, you will be well on the way to leading your life the way you want. However, fear sometimes remains as a huge stumbling block.

Take a minute. Relax quietly and reflect on any changes you may want to effect. What feeling appears to be the source of any anxiety you might experience? Is it fear? If so, how can you confront fears? Are your fears learned?

As I mentioned earlier, our fears are fears of loss of some kind. We can, of course, fear physical harm. For many women—too many—that fear is real. Ironically, however, other fears may impede those women from taking any action to eliminate their fear of physical harm.

The fear of loss has many disguises. It can be very apparent, of course, if we have experienced losses through death. But there can be other losses. We will examine these in more depth later, but I want to mention some of the ways you may be frightening yourself. You may harbor fear of rejection, fear of loneliness, fear of criticism, fear of losing your image or fear of change.

The biggest fear of all is the fear of change itself. Why? Perhaps it's because we, as women, don't have many prototypes for new behavior. At this point in women's history, there are daily challenges to the old ways, and at the same time, there are no new and easy definitions of how we should be.

Our roles have changed and are continuing to change. For many of us, being the provider is not a choice but a necessity. We can't risk the lure of the caught caretaker role—it has too many pitfalls and hidden angers. It's important for us to recognize the differences between the attitudes and the duties, to redefine caretaking into connecting, to describe self-actualization in the freeing words of *self-direction* and *self-support* and to acknowledge our own wants while at the same time being sensitive, accepting and flexible.

Challenging the Fears

We can define courage so that it includes any already-acquired skills that can help us challenge the fears. Courage is available if we emphasize our strengths instead of our weaknesses, if we recognize that any helplessness we might feel is learned and not inherited in our genes.

How can you help yourself to develop enough courage to challenge yourself to closely examine your shoulds, your caught caretaker role and your anger?

1. *You can give up blaming.* While it may be difficult to overcome any well-learned, one-down position, you can begin to accept your peer-level position with other women and with men.

2. *You can confront your fears in small steps.* Try a few risk-taking behaviors, such as saying quietly, but assertively, "I'm angry. . ." or "I'd like to have a quiet time with you." Avoid a self-applied requirement that you change immediately. Effective change takes time. Study. Talk. You can select one issue at a time. But watch that you don't keep your life in committee.

3. *You can calculate your risks.* Calculate the probable outcomes of living your life the way you want. Is it really as scary as you previously imagined? What are your skills, your talents? How can you handle another's questioning, criticisms or imposed shoulds? What could

be your losses? Do they outweigh the gains?

4. *You can remind yourself that honest expression of feelings enhances relationships.* You will be exhibiting trust in yourself and the other person. While expressing feelings may be difficult (such as saying, "I love you" after an argument, or "I'm sorry"), your self-worth will be reinforced in proportion to your risk taking.

5. *You can give yourself a chance.* Very few people die of not succeeding. Lack of success may be uncomfortable, even embarrassing, but it's usually not fatal. Trying and not succeeding is actually immensely instrumental to future successes if you allow yourself to learn from the experience instead of telling yourself you have failed and feeling guilt and shame.

6. *You can invest yourself in the changes you've decided.* Use your time and energy to explore what you want to do. Weave in your important self-determined values, principles and structure. Avoid confusing your values and principles with tasks.

Reassessing Your Shoulds and Wants

Now go back to your list of shoulds and wants. Have they taken on a new perspective? Can you determine the viability of your wants? Are they achievable? Are they really important? Does one stand out as more important than the others? Have you had the experience of wanting it for a long time? If you have, it's a real want instead of a passing fancy.

As you risk changing, as you move your shoulds into your want column, be sure to give yourself a lot of reinforcement. We all need a strong self-cheering section. Don't hold back feeling good about yourself.

You may have noticed that I don't use the word *dependency* much. There's a very good reason. I believe that female dependency is largely an *appearance* of dependency, a learned behavior characterized by the caught caretaker role, the suppression of anger and an allegiance to shoulds because of fears.

It's been my experience with women clients and group members that women are quite aware of the importance of relying on themselves. What is necessary is to *challenge* the old behaviors, *confront* the uncomfortable feelings and *allow* yourself the freedom of new lifestyles designed according to your own values, principles, desires and goals. By doing so you will be able to combine connecting and self-actualization.

Notes

1. Biofeedback is a technique that employs the use of various machines to help the patient recognize small physical changes, such as microvolts of electricity in muscles to which the machine is attached, or one-tenth of one degree change in hand temperature. These measurements are used to determine general physical stress and to help the patient learn methods of physical self-management. Combined with psychotherapy, biofeedback has proven to be very effective.

6

....

Manipulation

Manipulation is a communication pattern of people who perceive themselves to be without power. Small children are an example, as are those who don't understand or accept the concept of personal power. Perhaps because we learned as children that manipulation seems to succeed, we are reluctant to give it up when we're adults. But, more often, we aren't really aware that we're being manipulative.

Because *manipulation* sounds devious, some women will deny that they may be manipulative. Yet it's very unlikely that many women have escaped.

Why is manipulative behavior so hard to recognize? Probably because most of the time it seems natural. It is natural if you have limited yourself to the allowable feelings of love, grief, fear, guilt and shame. It makes sense if these feelings are common for you; if they are the feelings to which you respond; if they appear to be motivating feelings. Then you will "naturally" expect that others will react in the same ways you do, or at the very least, somewhat similarly.

Someone who is manipulative tries to achieve a desired result by attempting to incite fear, guilt, shame, love or affection. This desired result can be almost anything but it generally falls into the categories of getting someone else to behave in certain ways, getting someone else to do something specific or getting someone else to express love for the manipulator. The last objective—gaining love—is a very common reason for manipulative behavior.

Manipulation at Work

Let's go through a short scenario to help you recognize manipulative behavior and its results. Imagine yourself in this sequence.

A friend calls to invite you to lunch today. You hesitate to say yes, but since you refused her the last time, you decide to accept and ask where she would like to go.

She says, "I don't care," and throws the question back to you. You respond, choosing a restaurant you like. She is reluctant, but since that's where you want to go, she agrees.

STOP. What are you feeling now?

When you are seated, she complains about the table and the prices. You try to make her feel more comfortable by offering to pick up the check. After all, you did choose the restaurant. She refuses your offer.

About halfway through lunch, she asks you to help her with the charity campaign she's heading.

STOP. Now what are you feeling?

You are reluctant, using the excuse that you are too busy. She reminds you of a favor she did for you. You agree that she did do that, but you're still hesitant. She accuses you of not caring enough about her to be helpful to her cause. After all, it is an important charity.

By now, you are probably imagining yourself feeling *fear.* Initially, you were afraid to refuse her invitation because you might offend her. You had refused before. She would think you don't like her.

You also may be experiencing *guilt.* After all, *you* chose the restaurant, but she doesn't like it. It's *your* fault for choosing that particular place.

In addition, you probably are feeling *shame* because she did a favor for you and here you are—refusing to reciprocate for such a worthy cause. What kind of person are you anyway?

Reflect for a minute. How do you experience fear, guilt and shame? Physically? As anxiety maybe, intensified by headaches, stomach problems, lower back pain or insomnia?

Let's go back to the scenario and continue it briefly.

You refuse her plea for help.

Your friend leaves the restaurant—the one *you* chose—looking unhappy, very quiet, reminding you of her tremendous efforts; she gives you only a cursory goodbye. You return to the office or home feeling guilty.

But not for long, however, because sustained fear, guilt and shame can turn into anger and later into resentment—toward your supposed-to-be-friend. Manipulative behavior destroys relationships. It plays on feelings. Indirect, it undermines both self-worth and respect for others.

Using Love as a Manipulation Tool

Manipulative behavior is also very controlling because it uses the desire to love and be loved—the desire to connect—as a tool for manipulation. The manipulator can threaten another with a loss of love or friendship. She or he may also attempt to achieve results through an excess of love or friendship. Emotional blackmail becomes obvious when there is a threat of loss; bribery enters the picture when there is an excess of love and friendship.

Some common blackmail phrases are, "You don't care," "If you loved me, you would. . . ," "You're only thinking of yourself," "How can I love you when. . . ?" Common blackmail behaviors are silence, withdrawal, angry looks without verbal expression, moodiness and sexual refusal. Bribery may take the form of insincere compliments, insincere promises, extravagant gift giving and increased but deceptive sexual interest and responsiveness.

Why have we learned to manipulate and to respond to manipulation? *Because we have limited ourselves to the feelings of guilt, shame, fear and love and have rejected personal power.*

Disguising Anger to Manipulate

When we limit ourselves to the caught caretaker role, believing that we *must* be nurturing, caring, supporting, understanding and accepting to all persons all of the time, we express love through duties and very quickly become martyrs. For our martyrdom, we expect love and respect in return. We probably won't get what we expect but instead will experience lack of cooperation and maybe rejection if the persons around us have difficulty expressing their anger. Do you know any martyrs? What are your feeling reactions to them?

We limit ourselves by suppressing direct expressions of anger. It's not feminine to fight. We believe that if we're angry, we're bad, not caring, bitchy and crabby. We confuse the feeling of anger with angry behavior.

We are allowed, however, to be hurt, disappointed, grieved, upset, annoyed, disgusted or irritated. Hurt and disappointment are real feelings, of course, as you learned in Chapter 4, yet when the words are used to disguise anger, we try to change the responsibility for our reaction to the other person. This is manipulative behavior.

Imagine yourself being told by someone else, "I'm disappointed (grieved) by your actions." What feeling might you have? Guilt or shame? Maybe even fear of loss of their love or friendship? Try the same experiment substituting "hurt by" for "disappointed in." What's your reaction? The attempt is to make you feel guilt or shame or fear and therefore be responsible. The manipulator hopes you will then respond with behavior that he or she desires.

Recognizing Manipulative Behavior

Pay attention to how often you try to stimulate feelings of guilt or shame in another. Unfortunately, manipulation with guilt, shame and fear is a very common way we parent or have been parented. Take some time to reflect on how that statement may be true for you. You can learn from your experience, of course. You can watch for manipulation in your interactions now.

With children, manipulative behavior is quite common. They feel powerless, so they manipulate. If you, as a parent, are also manipulative, they will model after you, sensing your lack of personal power. On the other hand, when you speak directly, honestly and sincerely, manifesting the components of assertive communication, you are illustrating, thereby modeling, your personal power. You are also according children respect by interacting with them, no matter what their age. They will have high self-worth.

Asserting Rights vs. Manipulating

When we limit ourselves by imposing judgmental shoulds and self-criticism and restricting our choices of self-expression and creativity, we're frightened to break out of our predefined role expectations. Judging ourselves harshly ensures that we will do the same to others. They *should* behave in certain described ways (our way, of course). They *must* feel as we do (our feelings are the "right" ones).

When we impose shoulds on ourselves without examination, awareness and choice, as you read in Chapter 5, we reinforce low self-worth and consequent powerlessness. We limit ourselves by not recognizing, and thereby denying, our personal rights. If we believe that everyone but us is entitled to his or her rights—including the grocery store clerk and the taxi driver—the caught caretaker becomes dominant, putting the entire world, it sometimes seems, before herself or himself. Limitations such as these increase the feeling of powerlessness, leading us to believe that to gain what we want we must be indirect, that we must try to get others to be responsible by attempting to incite in them the fear, guilt, shame, love or affection we feel.

Included in the category of indirect interactions that are manipulative is blaming behavior. Whenever we point a finger, literally or by our words, we are attempting to get someone else to assume responsibility for *our* reactions.

Unfortunately, and too often, manipulation appears to succeed. If we abdicate self-management and responsibility, we will readily, "naturally," expect the same from others. A manipulative person believes, often unconsciously, that if others feel enough fear, guilt, shame or love—or any combination of those feelings—they will behave responsibly. They will do what they *should*. But will they?

Manipulation and Responsibility

Return to how you felt as you imagined the described restaurant scenario. Did you feel responsible? If you had been unaware of the caught caretaker role, you would have felt responsible because you subscribe to taking care of others, regardless of personal cost. Women have certainly learned to take care of others and be responsible for their reactions. What if they are upset or—even worse—angry? Then, of course, their reaction is *your* fault.

We have learned that we are responsible for others. Doesn't it make sense that we would also believe others are responsible for us? In addition, since we usually can guess reactions in others, it does seem as if we "made" them feel or respond. We often say, "You made me feel sad (glad, mad or scared)."

If we're perceptive at all, we can often determine fairly accurately in advance how others will respond. It does seem that we can "make" them feel, think and behave in certain ways. Imagine that someone says to you, "You look terrible in that color." What do you think your reaction might be? Perhaps anger or hurt? You might also determine that the speaker is envious of you or has some hidden motive for being so blunt. Your reaction will be based on your interpretation of the remark.

You are in charge of your actions and reactions. Understanding that no one can make you feel, think or behave in certain ways will enable you to gain personal power through self-management. It will also help you to comprehend that *you* cannot make anyone else respond in a prescribed manner. With that understanding, you can change being responsible *for* to responsible *to*. You'll be amazed at how much lighter you will feel. The only person you are responsible *for* is yourself. All others, you are responsible *to*.

Of course, small babies and toddlers require being taken care of. Yet, as they quickly grow, we can start being responsible *to* them in our roles as mother, teacher, caregiver and grandmother. Recognizing our responsibility *to* them will teach them responsibility *for* themselves, resulting in their high self-worth symbolized by good decision-making skills, faith in themselves and willingness to risk and create.

With peers, being responsible *to* involves deciding how you want to define the various roles you have assumed. Refer back to the role circle you drew in Chapter 2. Draw another, and again write job descriptions for each. Keep in mind changing responsibility *for* to responsibility *to*. Your interpretations of your roles may change dramatically.

Personal vs. Manipulative Power

It's extremely important that you not confuse personal power with manipulative power. There's no question that power gained through tapping another's feelings is strong. Think about how a child may appear very powerful through his or her manipulative behavior. You may have experienced your own upsetting responses with a child. Start observing interactions between people. When you identify manipulation, it's easy to see how manipulative behavior for people of any age can be powerful and at the same time destructive, leading to feelings of anger and resentment. Relationships may be maintained because of a professional relationship or family ties, but they are muddied by those indirect communications.

Remember, too, that personal power includes high self-worth and trust in and regard for yourself, plus an ability to extend trust and regard to your family, friends and associates. As you are teaching yourself behaviors that are assertive—direct, sincere and honest methods of communication—it will be necessary for you to be alert to well-learned old behaviors.

The Rewards of Direct Communication

Sometimes indirect communication patterns have been described as softer, more loving and kinder than direct communication, because direct communication has been confused with aggressive behavior. It is necessary for you to teach yourself ways to communicate that are assertive without being aggressive. There is a big difference, as you will see in Chapter 7, in which assertion, passivity and aggression are discussed in more detail.

Do not limit yourself to being a caught caretaker. Instead, recognize your choice to be nurturing, caring, supporting, understanding and accepting when you choose and to whom you choose. By doing this, you will be allowing yourself to give up fear, guilt and shame, the feelings closely associated with the caught caretaker.

You will avoid the consequences of others' mishandled anger and the resentment commonly experienced by the caught caretaker martyr.

You will recognize that direct, honest, sincere messages increase the possibility of love, affection, respect and friendship. Others will learn they can depend on you to say what you mean and to mean what you say. By allowing yourself to experience all of your feelings, recognizing them as feelings only and avoiding judging them as good or bad, right or wrong, you will be more aware of your abilities to communicate in the straightforward, honest patterns that reinforce your high self-worth and your respect and consideration for others. You will be opening for yourself and others the possibilities for a large variety of feelings, not limiting yourself and them to fear, guilt, shame and love.

Manipulation: Who Needs It?

It is becoming increasingly well established that women want to be both connecting and self-actualizing. In order to achieve both, it will be important for women to free themselves of destructive, controlling, manipulative behavior, as both giver and receiver. How can this be done?

Pay attention to your role definitions so that you are living life the way you *want* instead of the way others think you *should*. Examine your messages and select those that are appropriate for you now. That way you will be open to allowing others to do the same.

Permit yourself the freedom to express your personal rights. One man I know helped himself to be assertive, thereby not manipulative, by taping his list of personal rights to his shaving mirror. He testified that he stopped allowing others to infringe on his rights. He interrupted his caught caretaker reactions of fear, guilt and shame. He allowed himself to feel anger and to express his anger in behavior he considered to be appropriate.

Recognize that you are responsible only *for* yourself and responsible *to* others for the roles you have assumed. Then recognize that no one else is responsible for your reactions. You may have experienced, and be experiencing now, feeling reactions that are painful. It may appear that someone else has caused those reactions.

I am not trying to deny the existence of pain, hurt, disappointment, anger and grief because another has behaved in ways that affect us. Certainly each of us has known that experience. But the other person did not *make* us respond in the ways we did; we *chose* our reaction because of our values, principles, opinions and beliefs.

You have the personal right to express your opinions and values. Indeed, doing so may help someone else manage her or his life in a different way. Certainly, expressing yourself is a very positive self-management skill that can help you feel better and reduce your pain. Try to avoid inciting the feelings associated with manipulation; they can only cause an angry breach in your relationships.

In addition to teaching yourself to recognize your own manipulative methods, you can learn to recognize when you're being manipulated. You learn by examining your feelings, of course. When you are feeling fearful, guilty or ashamed, ask yourself if you have been the victim of manipulation. If you are unaware at first, but later experience anger and resentment, again question the interaction. It was more than likely manipulation and you allowed yourself to be the victim.

Recognizing that you have been manipulated will help you stop your own manipulative behavior. After all, who really *wants* to feel fearful, guilty or ashamed?

7

. . . .

Why Women Block
Assertive Behavior

D o you know the difference between *assertiveness* and *aggressiveness?* Many people confuse the two words. The confusion appears to be equal for both women and men, and the fear of female assertive behavior is present in both women and men.

How could that be when *assertive behavior builds high self-worth, enhances relationships and increases effectiveness?* One reason is that assertiveness and aggressiveness have been incorrectly interchanged, when, in fact, they are dramatically different. It's important that you understand the difference so that you can enjoy being assertive and reinforce your high self-worth and personal power.

Frequently an assertive women is described as unyielding, bitchy, nagging, selfish or thoughtless. Often these adjectives are used as a manipulation to keep a woman "in her place." They are used to incite a fear of rejection or loss of love. Since no one especially enjoys such labeling, a woman will sometimes shrink from assertive behavior, not understanding that assertive behavior is none of the above. She will retreat, especially if she is caught in the caretaker role; subscribing to shoulds, she is afraid to express anger and allows herself to feel only love, grief, fear, shame or guilt.

Women, Men and Assertiveness

Men who confuse assertiveness and aggressiveness will also be frightened by female assertiveness. They believe that their power will be challenged, that they will be dominated, that their lives will be adversely affected by loss of control or dominance and that they will appear to be a "Mr. Milktoast" to their cohorts. They may actually experience being shamed or ridiculed by other (frightened) men if they tolerate an assertive woman.

In addition, men have been taught to win, not to be equal. Their social conditioning emphasizes getting to the top of the ladder, achieving goals, producing a product, being superior, conquering sexually and avoiding failure. Meager, if any, attention is given to the expression of feelings. Feelings are for sissies. As little boys, males are encouraged to stand up for themselves, to say what they want and to work for what they want. They are taught assertive behavior.

But they are also taught to be competitive, sometimes fiercely, in their games and activities, and they are rewarded for strenuous physical sacrifices they make in order to be a "winner." Competitive games such as football emphasize aggressive behavior—overpowering, controlling, dominating, hostile, attacking, winning behavior. For this type of aggressive behavior, men are richly rewarded by both adulation and outrageous sums of money. This emphasis on winning is one reason there is so much confusion between assertiveness and aggressiveness for both men and women.

Males transfer the lessons they learn in competitive sports and in the military to business. In *Games Mother Never Taught You: Corporate Gamesmanship for Women*, Betty Lehan Harragan describes how men have assigned the techniques of games and war to the business world by commonly using such expressions as: "Welcome to the team," "Don't foul the play," "He quarterbacked the decision," "Follow the chain of command," and "Don't pull rank."[1]

Women generally have not learned these games. We have learned, instead, to play hop-scotch or jump-rope or house. We have felt pride if we were cheerleaders for the winning teams, if our boyfriends were the school jocks. Too often, instead of seeking the presidency, we have been content to be the secretary or the treasurer of the school class. And how often might we have disguised our excellent skills and abilities in order to allow a male to win or succeed?

But don't be hard on yourself if you have done these things. That is the behavior we have been taught as part of the caught caretaker role. The supportive position is a very important part of the caretaker role and, as you have seen, the caretaker is almost always present in women. Also, women have traditionally been taught passivity in many different disguises. Passivity is "feminine." Remember the words used to describe feminine? The caught caretaker role can appear to be passive. Suppressing, disguising or denying anger has passive components; being hurt or disappointed is passive.

Adopting predefined shoulds is passive. Manipulative behavior denies our personal power. Limiting ourselves to the feelings of guilt, shame and fear is passive. Our fear is passive when we deny our personal power because we are afraid of the consequences. Our fears are a major reason we limit assertive behavior. Women's fears—the fears of loss—can assume monstrous proportions, usually without our conscious understanding.

Assertiveness and the Fear of Loss

Unfortunately, for many people, loss is quite apparent in their lives. It may have included the death or desertion of a parent early in childhood, or the loss through death of someone who was extremely important: a sibling, intimate friend or lover. Most people suffer a variety of losses, many of which are not recognized as easily as death: they divorce, they lose their health, they move or important others move, they lose their job and security, they retire, they suffer robbery or destruction by war or nature. An unhappy childhood is an extremely significant loss, because one's childhood can never be recovered or replaced. Yet, women are not socialized to be alone or to tolerate loss, even though loss is inevitable.

The caught caretaker role limits valid displays of assertiveness, such as the expression of anger, because we're afraid that we will lose another's affection or love. Certain angry behaviors can be very destructive and frequently are, as you read in Chapter 4. For each person who has difficulty expressing anger, there are others who have equal difficulty receiving it. They will attempt to limit the feeling of anger and angry confrontations because of this difficulty. They will often attempt to assign responsibility to the person expressing the anger.

They think the angry person needs to control his or her feelings. Then everyone will be happy—a predefined should for every caught caretaker. We try to fit into the shoulds because we're fearful that to do otherwise will incite criticism or ostracism—in other words, loss.

There's a certain amount of reality in all of these concerns. Those close to us may appear to be insisting that we define ourselves traditionally as caretakers and fulfill our duties the way they want us to do. They limit their scope of options and they try to limit us.

Loss is real. No one can escape it, yet we often try by severely limiting our experiences and our risk taking because of our fears of loss. *We do not risk trusting ourselves, the most important self-management skill.* We are fearful of a true expression of feeling, an honest opinion, an important observation, a new path of action. Many people, seemingly immobilized by the fear of loss, do not permit themselves to be vulnerable. They will not permit connecting. No one can win without risking loss, and loss is part of life.

Rejection, a form of loss, is also very real. All of us at some time have experienced rejection. It may even have been at a time when we thought we were doing everything right. We were carrying out our duties, we were caretaking, we were suppressing or denying our anger and angry behavior, we were doing what we should, we were denying our personal power and he (she, they) *still* rejected us! Then we may see ourselves as victims, people to whom things just seem to happen. Sometimes that is the reality. We cannot control many of our losses, and we cannot ensure that others will not reject us.

But fearing loss and rejection inhibits assertive behavior. We often believe that if we become free caretakers, if we learn to express anger, if we examine our shoulds and if we give up manipulative behavior, we will lose all our acquaintances, friends and family. Sounds extreme, doesn't it? Yet many women believe this. Do you?

There is no question that the feelings that accompany loss and rejection are highly charged, traumatic and painful. When the feelings of grief seem to overcome us, we may become withdrawn, fearful of risking any further losses or rejections. Depression, anger, guilt, resentment and fear are all part of grief. It may be difficult to comprehend that you are grieving if you have not recognized losses other than death, but it's vital to understand that you do grieve when you incur almost any kind of loss or rejection. Without that understanding, you will allow yourself to become fearful, trying to avoid the painful feelings.

Not only is that avoidance impossible to accomplish, because some things do happen to us, but by attempting the avoidance we undermine our self-worth and reinforce a belief that life is difficult, painful and scary, and we had better not do anything (such as behave assertively) to risk loss or rejection.

Another important and inhibiting fear is the fear of change. Loss, rejection and change are closely connected because loss and rejection mean change of some kind, and change in turn has losses, even if it also means an improvement in one way or another.

Often people look back at change forced upon them and say, "I can see now it was for the best," but you can bet it didn't seem that way at the time. They would not have incurred the change if they had had a choice. With that understanding, you can comprehend how people will resist change. Change challenges one's skills, motivations, self-management and self-worth. Anyone who has ever voluntarily moved to a new community knows that, as does anyone who has gone back to school after many years away from studies or taken a different job or been promoted.

Voluntarily changing anything takes a lot of strength and self-confidence, a belief in yourself that you are capable of the challenges. Women are taught not to initiate challenges but, instead, to limit themselves to the caught caretaker role. They are also taught that self-actualization and connecting are opposites and that they can't have both.

Assertiveness and the Female Role

Many women who desire to be both self-actualizing and connecting believe themselves to be stuck *because they are female.* The ways they have learned this belief vary. Perhaps their mothers succeeded in professions considered to be traditionally male. The lesson the daughters were taught was that to be successful you have to be male or at least be in a male profession. (That is, male is superior.)

Or they may have observed a dominant father and a passive mother and readily understood that the father exercised the power. That looked appealing. Father may have encouraged his daughter to excel but also to remember she was a girl and women have certain duties. (Male is superior.) In addition, she may have learned skills and developed abilities, but what does she do with them? She has female duties to perform! (Male is superior.)

If there were brothers around, she probably observed and experienced firsthand that boys have more freedom and opportunities than girls. As she entered adolescence, she was further restricted because of her sex. (Male is superior.)

Women have seldom learned equality with males, so contemplating equality means contemplating changes in learned behaviors and feelings. What women most often have learned is to be passively supportive, in the variety of ways already discussed.

Fear and Risk

It is vital to your well-being and high self-worth that you understand what fears you may have learned. Otherwise, you will critically limit your behavior in order to be safe. *Trying to be safe and secure from loss curtails assertive behavior that has the potential to enhance connecting.*

Keep in mind that fear is an acceptable feeling for women. In addition to the fears already mentioned, women are afraid of winning or succeeding. Our lives are peppered with successes and failures—winning or losing a game, winning or losing a promotion, making or losing a deal, gaining or losing a relationship. It's interesting that what we term *failure* we also define as *losing*. We are fearful of losing prestige, status, respect, love and our own self-worth.

Winning means risking. There is no other way to win. Yet women are not taught to risk. We are taught to *please*, to fit in, to be a part of the larger (male) process, not to be the initiator, the leader or the innovator. We are taught to cheerlead and applaud the winning teams—usually composed of men or "aggressive" women —from the sidelines.

We haven't learned to appreciate our own skills and intelligence. We still hear the term "just a housewife." There are women who describe their very important job as "only a teacher's aide." Women continue to envy other women—in physical appearance, professional skills, accomplishments and even assertive behavior. But they remain unwilling to risk achieving the same things for themselves because *they do not trust themselves.* They have learned low self-esteem, fearing what the neighbors will think, how they will be judged or that they will be considered silly, uninformed, undereducated or naive. So they hide out, reinforcing their low self-worth by destructive messages such as, "That was stupid to do," "I'm really dumb," "I just haven't researched it enough" (keeping their lives in committee), "I know I'll fail (quit, look silly, etc.)" or "I'll try," which really means, "I won't because I'm not sure I can."

You can understand how the fear of failure and the fear of success have a common denominator: the fear of loss. Both failure and success can expose a person to ridicule, rejection, envy and harsh judgment.

Think about the fears you have. Accept them as learned and not inscribed in stone. Understanding yourself and accepting yourself are primary to initiating any change you may desire. You will be using high self-worth as the fuel for your life instead of as a goal down the road, yet to be reached.

Caretaker Subroles

Another reason women limit assertiveness is that they have well-learned subroles within the caretaker role. One of these subroles is the VOLUNTEER. I've enlarged the word to emphasize how many times you've been asked to do something voluntarily. What does voluntarily mean? Usually it means without pay, willingly, joyously, with enthusiasm, with sacrifice of time and with skill.

Please don't jump to conclusions—volunteers are

important people. They are vital to the welfare of society. But, a volunteer is a person who performs or gives services of her or his own free will.[2] A woman caught in her caretaker role will believe she *must* be available, that she *cannot* refuse. She can't say no.

Another subrole is that of the favor-giver, who can't refuse to do a favor when asked. "Will you do it just this one time?" "*Please* loan me your car (money, clothes, spare bedroom)!" If she did say no, she wouldn't be nice, caring, giving, strong, someone you can always count on, a good person, just a super gal, always willing to help.

Do these words fit you? If they do, ask yourself if you're saying yes instead of no because you believe you *must* instead of because you *want to*. It's a difficult distinction because women are socialized to be the givers, the volunteers, the nurturers, the encouragers and the supporters. We are socialized to say yes. That's positive. *No* is negative. Women aren't supposed to be negative. We aren't supposed to have "negative" feelings such as anger, resentment, jealousy, envy, rivalry or bitterness. We are taught to say yes. Indeed, much advertising is built on women's seeming inability to say no.

We are also taught the subrole of answer-giver, which obliges us to answer questions—*any* questions, no matter how personal, intrusive or inappropriate. Have you ever answered such a question and later asked yourself, "Why, on earth, did I answer *that*?!" Think about it for a minute. Have you found yourself revealing details that were meant to be private?

Within the caretaker is also the subrole of dutiful daughter. Parents can be demanding, especially if they believe they have sacrificed heavily for *your* needs. Now it is time for you to sacrifice for *their* needs. They may also have cared for their own mother or father and now it's your turn.

Parents may also have strong opinions about how you should be conducting your life. They are, of course, entitled to their opinions, but are they entitled to impose them on you? They often try to, usually through manipulation, so that you end up feeling guilty, angry and resentful.

Then, of course, there is the subrole of super-woman or supermom, about whom we have read so much. These women believe that in order to be okay, they must do *everything* well. They try to be volunteers, dutiful daughters, star athletes (or at least good), su-perlative housekeepers, gourmet cooks, marvelous lovers and accomplished professionals. They subscribe to the beliefs that home care is woman's work, mothers are more important than fathers, women hold mar-riages together and if they fail (lose), it's the woman's fault, and if their children have problems, it's the woman's failure (loss). If all doesn't go well, how do they feel? Guilty.

Guilt—Again

Guilt. There it is again—seemingly a woman's most prevalent feeling. We're guilty if it looks like we have made someone unhappy, sad, hurt or disappointed. We don't want to upset *anyone* by saying no. That often includes the department store clerk and the door-to-door salesman, as well as our best friends and our families.

How can we say no when we should be saying yes, so that everyone (supposedly including us) is happy? When we refuse to challenge the should messages we have received, we will continue to endure guilt if we actually do things differently. Why not place your wants and shoulds in the same column and do away with guilt, the token feeling, the inhibiting feeling?

Duties

We limit our options, the definitions of caring to the predefined descriptions, the duties. We limit ourselves to saying yes when we want to say no. We do this because we care about others. But this kind of caring, limiting ourselves, can require (according to the old rules) self-sacrifice, suppression of anger, denial of wants, avoidance of honest confrontation and expression of feeling, allegiance to shoulds and manipulative communication. In the process we may be reinforcing dysfunctional behavior in others.

If you love by trying to substitute the important characteristics of love with the duties you think symbolize love, you will discover that you are passive and subservient, always trying to put others ahead of yourself. The truth is that no one can do that. We might try. We might honestly believe we value others before ourselves. But attempting to do that will result in martyrdom without reward and will eventually contribute to both psychological and health problems, such as migraine headaches, insomnia, ulcers, obesity and years of built-up anger. Then we will use manipulative behavior to try to get others to do as we have done.

The Right—and Choice—to Be Assertive

All of the dynamics lead us as women to believe that we don't have the personal right to be assertive. The feelings of love, guilt, shame and fear, reinforced by overriding low self-worth, interfere with the right to act in our own best interests, to express our feelings honestly, directly and sincerely—in other words, to behave assertively.

Passivity

It's important to understand the differences between passivity, aggressiveness and assertiveness. Passivity implies that one is timid, shy, quiet and reserved. Passive people believe that to assert personal rights is overbearing behavior. They seem unable to act on their feelings—until they have had all they can take—then they act destructively (aggressively), unloading past angers, sometimes years old. Remember passive-aggressive behavior, described in Chapter 4?

They will also deny themselves in several ways. They will give credit to others, negating compliments and attention. They are uncomfortable with praise, yet they want it desperately. They are martyrs, suffering in silence, putting others first, pledging allegiance to the caught caretaker role. They are the peacemakers, accepting accusations, not wanting to upset anyone, working hard to see that no one else is unhappy, trying to smooth the feathers of everyone around them. They are anxious because they assume so many burdens. They have a lot to be concerned about. Of course, they do this all in long-suffering silence because they see themselves as helpless to initiate much change.

Although they may appear to be dependent, passive people will often use manipulation, an aggressive behavior. Using the passive position to incite guilt, shame and fear in others, they at the same time espouse love (giving in because they care about others), worry (they are fearful about others' abilities because they don't trust their own), guilt (their own guilt, they claim, for not doing what they should, especially excessive caretaking), fear (that someone else will be unhappy with them) and innocence (if only they had known. . .). If these behaviors don't work, they switch to passive-aggressive or passive-resistant behavior.

Passive people may also see themselves as the helpers, the healers and the nurturers, taking whatever anyone else hands out in order to keep the peace. They may honestly claim their passive behavior to be better than assertiveness, because they believe if they assert what they want, others might be upset or inconvenienced, feel rejected or be rejecting. Therefore, their passivity is hard to give up. They view passivity as desirable.

Passive people have low self-esteem; they have abandoned their personal power. They can be destructive to themselves as they try to absorb their own and others' anger when they are fearful and unaware of their potential to be assertive.

Aggressiveness

Aggressive people are identified as being domineering, autocratic, hurtful and attacking. They sometimes disguise themselves as passive people, so that they can manipulate by inciting love, fear, guilt and shame. We feel sympathy until we recognize the disguise. Manipulative people are aggressive people who are centered on what they want, but they try to obtain their goals indirectly and dishonestly. They are hurtful because of their indirectness. They are also anxious because they must be in control. The world is too threatening otherwise.

Openly aggressive people are easier to recognize. They are called "bullies." They must be in command. They will attempt to gain command through hostile language and behavior. They openly focus on their own

.1eeds, inflicting cruel words and behavior. They do not know how to handle their anger so they exhibit aggres-.ive behavior that is sometimes physically abusive. Their hostility hides insecurity with bravado and self-centered behavior.

Aggressiveness is based on low self-esteem. In order to value themselves, aggressive people find it necessary to put others down. They are usually oblivious to how others may judge them, because it's too dangerous to their shaky self-worth.

Both passive and aggressive people can appear to be powerful. But they can be successful only if you allow yourself to be intimidated by the feelings of guilt, shame and the fear of loss they try to inflict on you. Perhaps you rationalize your willingness to be intimidated by saying it's because you love the person who is behaving pas-sively or aggressively. However, it is very important that you question yourself as to why you really allow yourself to respond to such a person in ways that are destructive to you and to your relationships. Perhaps you will have found clues in the reasons stated above. Or perhaps you are in the caught caretaker role.

Assertiveness

By choosing assertive behavior you can become self-managing and exercise your personal power. Assertive behavior is:

Honest Be in touch with your feelings so that your ex-
Direct pressions and behavior are honest, direct and
Sincere sincere. At the same time, remember that it's
impossible to be totally objective about your-self. Be open to others' opinions and observa-tions.

LEARNED   The skills can be acquired. Read books that address assertiveness. Enroll in classes that teach assertive communication techniques. Do so with the understanding that the most important part of being assertive is believing that you have the right to act for yourself, to express yourself—in other words, to exercise your personal power.

SELF-ENHANCING   When you are assertive, you will be subtly saying, "I believe in myself and I believe in you and your ability to handle what I do and say." Assertive communication is the communication of peers. By acknowledging your own self-worth, you will accord respect to others.

In the beginning of the chapter, I stated that *assertive behavior builds high self-worth, enhances relationships and increases effectiveness.*

When you consider the alternatives, you can readily understand why I make such a strong statement. If you are caught in your caretaker role, you limit your options for caring, you substitute duties for characteristics, you allow yourself only love, fear, guilt and shame. You deny and suppress your anger. You do not allow yourself to creatively design your own life but instead subscribe to outside shoulds. And to achieve what you want, or think you want, you employ manipulative behavior, which results in resentment and alienation.

That behavior is not too attractive, is it? It certainly is an obstacle to your being connecting and self-actualizing. However, behaving assertively can help you achieve both goals. Behaving assertively can help you understand that connecting and self-actualization are not incompatible; they can be achieved concurrently.

Managing Fear and Listening

Don't allow yourself to be manipulated by the adjectives used to incite your fears of loss. Everyone has fears to some degree and they are easily triggered because loss is painful. But you can manage the fears so that they do not become dominant and inhibit self-actualization. By recognizing your fears, you will be able to more effectively manage your reaction. *Worry is fear in advance.* You worry that you can't handle what might occur. The act of worrying magnifies the feelings of fear, yet some women believe that if they worry they are better caretakers.

The truth is that *you cannot be connecting when you are fearful or when you subscribe to predefined caught caretaker roles. The caught caretaker is not effective at connecting or self-actualization.*

I'm well aware that this statement can be debated by those who cling to traditional ideas and beliefs, but I do not hesitate to state it strongly because I have observed too much unacknowledged anger, too much built-up resentment and too much fearful martyrdom. As women, socialized for our roles, we have learned to curtail our exploration, to put ourselves into second or third or fourth position on our own totem pole, to inhibit our feelings and our reactions. As a result, we risk losing the very things we are most fearful of losing: our connecting qualities (they are replaced by anger and resentment) and all our important others (manipulation is alienating and martyrdom is boring).

Assertive behavior takes many different forms. Being assertive means not only being able to state your own position or feelings. It means listening carefully, so that you are able to understand what another person is saying. Often we are too busy trying to figure out what we will say to appear intelligent, make an important point or defend ourselves. Contrary to popular interpretation, listening is not a passive activity. When you listen carefully and attentively, you are subtly telling the other person that you respect his or her opinion and trust yourself enough to listen carefully so that when you do respond, it will be relevant.

Assertive behavior is basically a symbol of belief in yourself that you are worthy of your personal rights, that you can exercise your personal power and that you are capable of both connecting and self-actualization. Behaving assertively is a skill, a method that can be learned, but the technique will fall flat without high self-worth as the most important factor.

Notes

1. Betty Lehan Harragan, *Games Mother Never Taught You: Corporate Gamesmanship for Women* (New York: Warner Books, 1977).

2. William Morris, ed., *The American Heritage Dictionary of the English Language* (Boston: Houghton Mifflin Co., 1969).

8

. . . .

Jealousy, Envy and Rivalry

Y ou can understand by now that women easily experience love, guilt, shame and fear. Anger is
more difficult to acknowledge (sometimes impossible, it seems), as are feelings of jealousy, envy and
rivalry.

Of course, we all know that women do feel these
feelings. But since the feelings are uncomfortable, we
try to get rid of them. Sometimes we blame someone
else for making us feel jealous, envious or competitive.
They shouldn't act that way or have what we want or try
to be better. We can react by trying to downgrade others
or their accomplishments in order to handle our own
feelings. At other times we chide ourselves for feeling
the feelings at all; they are bad feelings, and we decide
we are bad for having them. We label ourselves inse-

cure. We tell ourselves that if we really felt okay about who, how and what we are, we would not feel jealous or envious or competitive.

Whenever you try any of the behaviors described above, what are you doing? You're denying your personal power. You're denying your self-management abilities. You're denying your high self-worth.

It's important to understand the differences between jealousy, envy and rivalry because the three feelings are similar.

Comparing Jealousy, Envy and Rivalry

Psychologist Rita Vuyk in *The Encyclopedia of Sexual Behavior* states that *jealousy* results from the fear of losing something to a competitor, *envy* arises when someone else has something we want or is allowed to do something forbidden to us, and *rivalry* is the desire and effort to do better than someone else.[1] Everyone feels these feelings sometimes. They are not bad feelings, and we are not bad people when we have them. Women, however, will feel jealous, envious or competitive often because they have been conditioned to feel that way.

How have women learned to be jealous, envious or competitive? Reflect back to what you read in Chapter 1. There aren't many women who are satisfied with their bodies. Do you sometimes wish you were like someone else, or that you acted as she does? Is that wishing the same as feeling envy? Do you think the advertising messages, especially about personal products designed to enhance us, encourage competitiveness or envy?

Adolescent girls compete—for adolescent boys, among other things. Can you recall any feelings you might have had as a teenager? How did you rate in your group? Or were you even *in* the group? Did you suffer because you viewed yourself as too plump or too thin? Too dumb or too smart? Compared to whom?

Jealousy is actually encouraged in many ways. Do you recall your early courting days? Or your adolescent relationships, both with boys and girls? As adolescents, we were *supposed* to be jealous. The belief was that if you didn't behave jealously, you really didn't care. Sometimes you might even have made up situations so that you could prove to yourself that you were loved because another person, your girlfriend or boyfriend, would react jealously. Then you would quickly reassure them that you really did care about them above all others. You couldn't take a chance that they might actually withdraw. It was a game, but it taught jealous feelings. The game reinforced jealousy as an expression of caring. Another learned fear of loss.

Learning rivalry or competitiveness is considered a sign of being well motivated. As you know, in our society, accomplishments, talents, skills, economic and social status and possessions are highly valued. You can see very easily how competitiveness is encouraged in every facet of our lives.

Learning Jealousy, Envy and Rivalry

How did you learn rivalry as a child? Through competing for grades? Looks? Reading skills? Do you remember all the names given to reading groups indicating the reading level? Everyone knew what all the names represented, even though the levels were supposed to be disguised.

Parents reinforce rivalry in a variety of ways, sometimes quite innocently. They are honestly proud when their children succeed. They encourage their children to do their best. Unfortunately, there's no easy answer to the dilemma. Parents want their children to be successful and to do their best. Competitiveness is a reality parents face every day—on the job, especially. Perhaps it's a good thing to teach competitiveness. Yet, children can feel low self-esteem when they don't make the team, when they aren't chosen, when they are encouraged to be the "best."

You can quickly understand by those few examples how our cultural mores encourage jealousy, envy and rivalry. Remind yourself when you have these feelings that they are feelings, not behaviors, and feelings are acceptable. The way we choose to respond determines the behaviors.

There are other, more complex ways people learn to feel jealousy, envy or rivalry. As we examine a few, think about how you may have had similar experiences.

You may have felt a lack of love during your childhood. The deprivation may have seemed very real and very extreme. Your message from the past might have been, "You're not lovable." Love may have existed even though it wasn't expressed in ways that were meaningful for you. You might understand the dynamics now, and you may have a great deal of love expressed in your life now, yet you may still occasionally experience the feelings you had as a child. Being jealous of your loved ones may be a problem in the present, or there may be times when you think nobody loves you. How could they? Your self-image seems at an all-time low. Then envy may be added to jealousy.

During your childhood, you may have lost an important person: a parent, a sibling, your best friend—someone you greatly loved. Not understanding the feelings of grief, you might have felt a supreme loss that you believed could never be recovered. You looked around and saw that other children still had both parents, families, best friends. You might easily have been very jealous if you believed there was any threat of further loss. You might have been fearful that your remaining parent would remarry and you would lose her or his love to another. You might have felt envious of all those other nice, natural families. You may still be coping psychologically with that loss, jealously guarding your present family.

As a child you may have felt strong sibling rivalry. Why couldn't you do as well as your sister or brother? Your sister was beautiful; you were cute. Your brother got to do all the fun things; you had to help mother. First come, first served is often the rule in big families. Hand-me-downs can be both desirable and awful. Jealousy, envy and rivalry can all be experienced in such a setting.

If you were an only child, you might have looked around at larger families and wanted what you thought they had. You may have hung around their homes a lot, trying to absorb the life-style that you believed was more desirable than your own. They seemed to have so much fun, and you were so lonely. Or you may have lived in a large family and believed you were lost in the crowd. Then you envied the only child.

You may have been parented in such a way that now it's difficult for you to feel high self-esteem. Your parents may have been critical, believing that criticism is motivating. They may have taught you to be fearful of rejection and change, magnifying your fear of loss, and leading you to inhibit risk and assertive behavior. You may have learned that passivity is correct for little girls (and grown women). You may have been told no, no, no instead of being encouraged to explore your environment and your potential.

As an adult, you may have lost your companion of many years. This type of traumatic loss can result in feelings of jealousy that are not well understood. As you begin to rebuild a life that includes new people, you will feel jealous if you think there is any possible risk of loss or rejection. You may never have experienced jealousy in your previous relationship. Your jealousy now is directly related to your fear of all the feelings that accompany loss.

If you have lost a child, you may jealously guard against losing another, not only to death but also to a relationship or any change that may appear to be a loss to you, such as a move away from home.

Looking at these examples, both simple and complex, you can realize that in all of them the stage is set for learning to feel insecure, fearful and disadvantaged.

Byproduct Feelings

Do you feel insecure, fearful and disadvantaged because: You were orphaned? Or poor? Or not pretty? Or unloved? Or lonely? Or fearful? Because you are Black? Or Asian? Or gay? Or Catholic? Or Jewish? Because you are a woman? The list reminds me of one of those funny cards—the start of the sentence is the same for a variety of different endings with a check box beside each for your choice. In this case, each woman has her own individual boxes to check, in addition, of course, to the last.

Women have indeed suffered disadvantages. We can credit the feminist movement for raising our consciousness about the inequalities, and we can be proud of ourselves when we take advantage of our opportunities now. Forget blaming and downgrading—that reduces personal power and accomplishes nothing.

Understanding how you might have learned to feel disadvantaged can be helpful. It will be freeing when you accept the understanding and decide to apply your insights to help you achieve changes you want. Believing oneself to be disadvantaged can easily lead to feelings of insecurity and fear, and those feelings can lead to jealousy, envy and rivalry. Being caught in the caretaker role can also lead to the same feelings of insecurity and fear, as you have seen. Can a caught caretaker allow herself to acknowledge jealousy, envy or rivalry? Of course not, because she believes that to do so would be noncaring.

But a caught caretaker requires caretakees. What if she loses them? The threat of losing can be real or imagined, but the impact is the same in either case. She feels jealous. She fears loss.

Does the fear of loss inhibit assertiveness? Can jealousy and envy lead to anger? The answer is yes, to both of these questions. If we allow our fears to be overpowering, we may behave quite nonassertively. Feeling jealous, envious and insecure, we retreat. We don't try to compete. We believe we don't have a chance to win anyway, and we don't examine our unwillingness to risk.

Then how we suffer, because we know that loss and rejection hurt. Feeling jealous and envious is painful—not bad, but painful.

On the other hand, we may behave aggressively, hoping we can hold on to whomever or whatever we are fearful of losing. We become possessive, grasping and constricting. We feel fearful that our loved one—husband, lover, child or friend—will find someone better than we believe ourselves to be. So we try to restrict *their* behavior instead of acknowledging our own fears and taking the risks involved to confront them. When we try to restrict (control) another's behavior, and it doesn't work, we become angry. You can see how all of our feelings are a complex mixture. Sometimes it's very hard to tell exactly what is occurring.

Societal Pressures

There is little doubt that today's society has elements that stir up feelings of jealousy, envy and rivalry. The pressure of materialism is hard to resist. We are encouraged to better ourselves with housing, automobiles, clothing, jewelry, travel and appliances. In addition, the standard of living you desire may be difficult to achieve without two incomes or one large one. As a consequence, you may envy others who seem to have it easier.

With the push to achieve professionally, the emphasis is on performance. When we see someone else getting ahead, we feel insecure; maybe we can't accomplish as much as we see others doing.

Sexual jealousy is sometimes seen as instinctive and universal, but that is far from the truth. Sexual jealousy is a product of a society that provides limited possibilities for sexual gratification, and that emphasizes close attachments between couples. Sexual exclusivity is both taught and preached, and the so-called "sexual freedom" of the 1960s and 1970s has been dealt a death blow by the increase of sexually transmitted diseases. Therefore, given the slightest provocation, a person struggling with insecurities will feel sexual jealousy.

Women, generally, tolerate sexual infidelity more easily than men do. Men will not usually endure the infidelity because it is a blow to their self-esteem, which may be closely tied to their sexual ability. Women who engage in various sexual interactions are labeled "promiscuous," and criticized. Men are called "studs," and are often admired, mostly by other men. Men who have mates who are sexually unfaithful are "cuckolded," but there is no equivalent word for women in the same situation.

Society trains women to be the caretakers, the professional hard workers, the loving and faithful wives, the backbone of the home. Women often try to achieve these ends through great personal sacrifice. They are encouraged and reinforced because they are "strong," "understanding," "accepting," "long-suffering."

You can begin to understand how jealousy (a fear of loss), envy (a desire for something more or something forbidden) and rivalry (the quest for the best) are, in fact, learned in our society. But women have difficulty accepting the feelings because they are "bad" feelings.

For men, those feelings are acceptable. If a man is jealous, his mate must be doing something or behaving in some way that is threatening to him. It's her responsibility. If a man is envious, it's because he wants only the best for himself and his family. If a man is competitive, he's well motivated. If a woman feels jealous, envious or competitive, she's insecure.

Women and Insecurity

It's a common belief that a woman's insecurity is the root of her "problem." There's little, if any, recognition that women are in many ways taught jealousy, envy and rivalry. Of course, the truth is that women can have well-learned insecurities. We can have well-defined caught caretaker roles, prescribed shoulds, well-developed manipulative behaviors and enormous fears of loss.

When we do not question the definitions, the shoulds and the fears, so that we can develop for ourselves the ways we *want* to be, we really do gamble with our lives. The prize (?) can be insecurity and guilt (there it is again). We think we're not accomplishing. Perhaps we can't accomplish. Or, perhaps we aren't doing whatever we should be doing enough or correctly. We must keep trying harder.

The result of that type of martyrdom is that we don't believe we are appreciated enough. Since we have indeed made a gigantic sacrifice, it may be true that there can never be enough appreciation. Then we resent those we believe have caused the feelings. We are trying to give away the responsibility for ourselves and our reactions. We see ourselves as victims. Feeling victimized, we reinforce the insecurities; we become disheartened, immobilized and incapacitated. These feelings may result in illness, chemical dependency or depression. If we allow ourselves to admit that we feel jealous, envious or competitive, we quickly add that we're not really very nice.

What is really the bottom-line feeling here? Could it be anger?

It could be, or it could be a deep-level, unconscious knowledge that you don't want to feel insecure. There are many good things about you. You really are pretty nifty. You want to believe that. On the other hand, perhaps you aren't too sure, especially if your message from the past is negative.

Insecurity is difficult to unlearn. No one can talk you out of it, because it's a feeling about yourself. Many people work hard to reinforce their bad feelings about themselves. The belief that you can't achieve personal power may be so well learned that you think you were born that way. "That's just the way I am" is a phrase you may often repeat, but it indicates a reluctance to change or to challenge yourself.

Yet, it is possible to change when you decide to give yourself the opportunities of self-awareness, self-management and personal power—high self-esteem.

Have you ever *seriously* considered believing that if someone doesn't like (love, accept) you, it's her or his loss? If you have, you're on the right track. You are acknowledging your worth as a person. You are managing your insecurities.

You can flip over your coin that has the fear of loss on one side. The other side is your desire to be loving and to be loved. Have you ever considered that? The other side of the fear coin is connecting.

There's a whole world of difference between (a) believing yourself to be worthy and capable of love and confidence and (b) hiding out, uncomfortably conscious of your jealous and envious feelings and, at the same time, trying to disguise them with blaming and nagging about what others are doing wrong.

You can easily understand that to blame and to put down others inhibits both connecting and self-actualization. We are most likely at be envious of someone who is similar to us. For example, not knowing anything about physics, I can feel glad when a physicist friend wins a prize or an award for her accomplishments. It's harder when a colleague in psychology is awarded a prize.

There are some who believe that envy and jealousy lead to rivalry or competitiveness and that that is good motivation. I do not agree with the theory, because envy and jealousy are founded in feelings of disadvantage and insecurity. I believe that if one is actually feeling envy and jealousy, he or she will either retreat (nonassertive behavior) or attack (aggressive behavior). The attacking may be wrongly identified as rivalry.

If you are truly competitive, you will see yourself as equal, and worthy of attaining the prize or job; and should you not gain what you want, you will simply be disappointed. You will still be motivated to risk or try again. In addition, because you feel good about your efforts and yourself, you can feel glad about another's gain, even in your disappointment. (It's important not to confuse envy with righteous indignation. If someone else has cheated or lied or won by improper or illegal methods, you will feel faulted and angry. That's not envy.)

Recognizing and Managing Jealousy, Envy and Rivalry

How can we best manage these feelings of jealousy, envy and rivalry when we, as women, have been subjected to many different forms of indoctrination? By claiming for ourselves the very things we often deny ourselves: personal power, self-management and high self-worth.

We can allow ourselves to recognize that we sometimes feel jealous, envious and competitive. We aren't bad people when we have these feelings. Recognizing the feelings provides us the opportunity to choose appropriate behavior. We do not *have* to react in ways that are destructive to the very goals for which we strive: connecting and self-actualization. We can initiate change if we choose. The method remains the same—following the five steps for change:

1. *Gain awareness* through introspection, investigation and understanding.
2. *Decide how you want to handle yourself.* Decide, in advance, how you will behave when you experience envy and jealousy.
3. *Confront your fears of loss.* Believe in yourself, your understandings and your decisions.
4. *Behave differently.* Remind yourself of the circular pattern of behavior, feelings, thinking, behavior, etc.
5. *Reinforce yourself* for your understandings, your acceptance and your new behavior. It may not be easy as you change your patterns, but it will certainly be rewarding.

Change doesn't occur overnight or with one trial. Change takes practice. If you find yourself using former behaviors, accept it, and realize that recognizing what you're doing is in itself a gain. It's not easy to relearn old lessons or handle old messages that have been strongly reinforced, but it is possible—if you want to.

Notes

1. Albert Ellis and Albert Abarbanel, eds., *The Encyclopedia of Sexual Behavior* (New York: Jason Aronson, 1983), p. 567.

9

. . . .

Compliments and Criticisms

Are you comfortable when you tell someone what you've accomplished? Do you relate a compliment you've received? Are you proud of a prize you've won or a goal you've attained? Do you tell yourself you look great today?

If you readily answered yes to the questions, it's likely that you don't have difficulties with compliments. You're also in the minority. So many women do have problems accepting compliments that the subject warrants a close look.

If you want to conduct an informative exercise, ask a group of women to compliment one another, one at a time, and in some order. Then ask each one to tell how she felt giving a compliment and how she felt receiving one. How was the compliment delivered and received?

Was there eye contact? Was there blushing? Did anyone feel anxious? Were the compliments superficial, that is, about appearance and clothing? Were they easier to give than to receive? Why? It's an interesting exercise and one that will quickly illustrate the difficulty women have with compliments. And we thought we only had problems with criticism.

Compliments and the Caught Caretaker

What kind of woman finds complimentary behavior particularly difficult? By this time, you're sure to answer, "the caught caretaker," and you're correct. But caught caretakers give lots of compliments. Of course. Since we all like to hear nice things about ourselves, we will respond warmly to someone who tells us nice things. We may even love that person, or at least like her or him. The caught caretaker achieves her goal.

She may also believe that another person is dependent upon her approval, and if she has successfully built dependence in someone else, she will be correct.

There's the likelihood that the caught caretaker believes her compliments to be entirely correct, true, sincere and honest. But if she is able to examine her motives very carefully, she may discover that she is using complimentary behavior as a manipulation tool to stimulate love feelings that are directed back to her.

No matter how easy it is for the caught caretaker to give compliments, receiving them is an entirely different matter. She may want them desperately, but it's not okay to get them. What a terrible conflict. Her self-worth depends on others' approval of her caretaking, but because she is caught, she will be unable to clearly acknowledge her desire to be complimented.

The caught caretaker has pride confused with personal power, self-management skills and high self-worth. She may well believe that pride is destructive if she defines pride as an excessively high opinion of herself, perhaps conceit or arrogance. I agree. Conceit and arrogance are not desirable characteristics for anyone. But pride can also be defined as valuing or believing in oneself—having, in other words, high self-worth.

There is one instance, however, when the caught caretaker believes that pride is okay, even desirable. That's when the pride is supposedly in someone else: "I feel proud of your accomplishment (that you're my daughter, that you're my husband, that you won)." The pride only *looks* secondhand; the real meaning is, "I did my job well and you and I succeeded."

It's also okay for the caught caretaker to receive compliments directly about how well someone she caretakes has done. Again, while she may indeed be very glad for another's accomplishments, if she is caught in her caretaker role, she will also be very proud of the person in a possessive manner. She will see herself as the power behind the throne, as the self-sacrificing mother or as the invaluable assistant of the auxiliary to the *real* authority (such as women's auxiliary groups to all-male organizations).

Taking the credit for a child's accomplishments can become a habit that is difficult to break. Diane, a client who has looked hard at her caught caretaker role and changed a lot of her behavior, told me that a friend complimented her son, saying what a great guy he is. Diane stopped herself before she said, "Thank you," and then she said, "I think so, too."

Compliments and Self-Image

But even if you aren't a caught caretaker, you may still have problems receiving compliments. Why? For clues to any discomfort you may have, remember that compliments, except from someone who knows you very well, are usually about your appearance or your achievements. These are part of your self-definition.

Go back to your definition of *feminine*. Did you use any words that suggest modesty? You may believe that humility shows refinement and good taste. There's also the possibility that you believe that modesty is polite. To go even further, you may believe that immodesty is vanity and that to be vain is to be aggressive.

There may be some truth to the last belief if you define vanity as *excessive pride* or *conceit*. Then, to be vain would be to be aggressive, but there is a difference between being aggressive and being assertive enough to have pride in yourself. Then you can experience the joy inherent in your high self-worth, the joy that enhances your connecting and self-actualization.

If you say, "I don't have any beliefs like the ones suggested, and I still have problems with compliments," you may be harboring a poor physical self-image. Think back to Chapter 1, on the subtle (and not so subtle) putdowns. Your self-image could be so poor that you cannot allow yourself to believe *any* compliments about your person—except, maybe, those that agree with your own analysis of yourself.

Compliments about your achievements are difficult to accept if you have learned that it's important to be unpretentious and to recognize that many people have contributed to your successes and *they* deserve credit—or if you have learned to undervalue yourself because you are a woman.

Particularly in the business world, women believe that they must work harder in order to be equal. "If you want a good job done, find a busy woman" is a true axiom. Women themselves reinforce this belief and they are willing to work harder, longer and for less pay when they are unable to place as high a value on their contributions and leadership abilities as on those of men.

A woman must think well of herself before she can believe compliments about her achievements, personal appearance or personality. No one can talk you out of a low opinion. The effort is an exercise in futility. The woman who undervalues herself will refuse the compliments even though she may want them desperately: "What? This old thing?" "Everybody helped." "It wasn't an original idea." "Anybody could have done it." The person paying the compliment may feel embarrassed or even put down, and wonder, "Why did I bother?"

The Danger of Comparing

How might you have learned to be nonaccepting of your achievements? It probably started with comparisons. We learn to undervalue both ourselves personally and our achievements when we compare ourselves or are compared unfavorably with others.

Comparison starts within the family unit, and everyone experiences it to greater or lesser degrees. If you learned that you just weren't quite up to par, or if your message from the past is negative, it will be difficult now for you to be self-accepting or to believe in your abilities. Norma, a woman in her early forties, still struggles with her message of, "You won't be able to handle it" (whatever "it" was). Decisions are very hard for her to make.

If there was family emphasis on particular abilities, such as intellectual skills, and you believed you didn't measure up, you might be able to accept compliments about other abilities, but not about your intellectual capacity. If you were unfavorably compared to a sister or brother or cousin, you can continue to hang on to the unfavorable comparison right up to the present, and downgrade your accomplishments.

The Fear of Succeeding

It will be even more difficult to accept your successes if you believe that being more successful than someone you love is the same as saying, "I don't love you." If that is your belief, you won't want to risk at all. Or if you do risk and succeed, you won't allow yourself to acknowledge your successes. How could you? You feel very guilty and you think the loss is too great.

An example of this belief was illustrated by Betty, a woman in her late thirties. An intelligent and skillful professional, she could not understand why when she attained prominence and high regard in her field, she would not accept advancements—advancements that would mean different responsibilities and greater rewards, including a higher salary and public recognition. She had even changed jobs to avoid such situations. But the advancement offered to her that prompted her to come to my office was "too good to turn down," and she wanted to understand her rejecting behavior. Betty finally comprehended that she believed her success might be perceived by her poorly educated, but very loving, parents as a put-down, almost like telling them, "I don't love you." The specter of the loss was frightening.

To challenge such a fear, ask yourself if you are measuring self-worth by what you do instead of who you are. When you are able to measure your self-worth by who you are, you will use the same measurement for loving others. Then achievements assume their proper position, and you won't be fearful of risking and succeeding. Rather, you will allow yourself opportunities for achieving. In Betty's case, she also knew after close examination that her parents wanted her to succeed, that they were loving and supportive. Her fears were self-imposed.

But if achieving was discouraged for women in your family unit, you may have learned "the waiting game." To win the game, so that you could become a caught caretaker, you had to play by the rules: Don't try for a career because you won't use it—unless it's a career you can fall back on if your husband dies. Don't achieve more than a man or he will feel threatened. Don't acknowledge any successes you accidentally have; that would be unfeminine. If you learned the game according to those rules, it will be impossible for you to assertively claim your gains as your own. Any compliments you receive will be perceived as threats and will reinforce your fear of loss.

There's also the possibility that you received a mixed bag of instructions. On the one hand, you were encouraged to learn and perform, taught to do "masculine" things. Your father, particularly, may have been very proud of you. On the other hand, he may also have taught you that you must remember that because you are a girl, as a woman your real job will be caretaking (as a caught caretaker). As a woman, you should behave like one. Limit yourself; don't boast; don't be aggressive; give other people credit instead of yourself.

The fear of succeeding was likely not limited to your family situation. It existed in school, on the playing field, during musical recitals and at dancing school. As an adolescent, you may have been scared to succeed, because you didn't want to stand out, be different.

Women are more often fearful of succeeding than they are of failing. When people fear failing, they will work hard to avoid it. When they are fearful of succeeding, they will not allow themselves to succeed. They view success as presenting more responsibilities than they can assume. They must constantly keep up an effort; they don't trust themselves enough to believe they can sustain the success. Too often, these lessons are what women have been taught. How can we receive compliments about our achievements if we are fearful of those achievements?

Now, however, it is time to mobilize your self-management skills. It's helpful to understand how you might have learned to undervalue yourself and your accomplishments. But those experiences, whatever they were, don't provide an excuse for continuing to reinforce low self-worth. You cannot allow low self-worth to prevent you from reaching your goals of connecting and self-actualization.

Criticisms

It's almost easier to be criticized than to be complimented. Criticisms we can believe—they fit right into our value system if we undervalue ourselves. And, of course, we can give ourselves additional critical messages, concentrating on our "bad" performance or our "awful" appearance. We really don't need anyone else's criticisms when we criticize ourselves so much.

All the reasons outlined above about why women have difficulty receiving compliments are the same reasons why women are so self-critical. Of course, we don't enjoy being criticized by others. Who does? Yet, it's easy for women to buy into the critical remarks, accepting them as truth, no matter the source. More important is that we interpret criticism as rejection, and that activates fear of loss.

Even though it is sometimes tempting to be critical of others, to be critical—to even feel critical—is fear-producing. Again the fear of loss is overwhelming. To be critical of others is to risk reinforcing their low self-esteem, and they will work hard to avoid you. It's the same when you criticize yourself; you reinforce your low self-esteem. But you can't avoid yourself.

You tell yourself that your opinion doesn't count anyway, so why speak up? If you have an opinion that's different, you must be wrong. Yet on a feeling level, believing yourself to be wrong or imperfect or lacking becomes absolutely tiresome. Then you feel angry. But since anger is not acceptable, you downgrade yourself even more or become openly critical in an attempt to feel okay about yourself. Your behavior evolves into a vicious destructive circle.

How can you stop such destructive behavior? First, remind yourself of your own high self-worth. Your belief in yourself will determine the extent to which you will be able to handle outside criticism. Through high self-worth, you will stop destructive self-criticisms. You will enable yourself to focus on what is being said instead of on the anxiety and anger you may feel. You will be able to carefully determine whether the criticizer has any validity for you. Is he or she someone who knows you well enough to judge? What is the basis of the criticism? Perhaps jealousy or envy? Or anger?

Second, don't criticize either yourself or others. Instead, learn to speak assertively. To say only what is wrong or imperfect or lacking solves nothing. To tell yourself or others what you want, or how you want it done, or how to improve, will get the job done. And everyone feels better. There's no risk of loss with assertive behavior.

Many people believe that to criticize is to motivate. Quite the opposite occurs. Sometimes, on the surface, it may appear that people who are criticized will try more diligently, but they never quite believe in themselves. They aren't too fond of the criticizer, either.

In some families, criticism is a way to avoid intimacy. It becomes a way of life that resembles quicksand. The family members cannot risk standing up and being counted, because they will sink. They become critical of others in order to attempt to feel good about themselves. But it doesn't work.

In other families, criticism is a common communication style and the family members may learn to interpret *every* remark as a criticism. One of my clients who grew up with a lot of criticism couldn't understand that she did this. One day, to prove to her that she did indeed interpret remarks as criticisms, I said to her, "Where did you get that blouse?" Her quick reply was, "What's the matter? Don't you like it?"

Feeling, Thinking and Criticism

There's one other very important dynamic of criticism to examine. Every person has both feelings and thoughts. These motivate the behavior, as you saw in the wheel figure. In our society, thinking is highly valued. Logic is gold. Feelings, however, are often judged to be irrational.

If you are a predominantly "feeling person," you may be criticized for being irrational. You may even criticize yourself. You will be accepting the belief that thinking is superior. However, neither feeling nor thinking is superior. We all do both, sometimes doing one more than the other. However, both feeling and thinking are desirable and necessary for us to be fully aware persons. One mode is not better than the other.

Women are very often more feeling. If you perceive yourself as a feeling person, value your characteristics as being equal to thinking. Don't permit yourself to be criticized for being irrational.

So how can we benefit ourselves and others? With compliments. We're right back to where we started. Compliments that are sincere, honest and direct (sounds like the definition of assertive behavior) can help reinforce confidence, security, love and high self-worth. You can learn to give them to yourself and to others. They aren't the whole solution—only high self-worth is—but they can help.

10

. . . .

Sensuality and Sexuality

Have you ever considered the definition of *sensuality*? Looking at the word can be helpful. The meaning is right there: senses—sight, hearing, smell, touch and taste. Sensuality employs the senses to allow us to live fully in the world.

Taking into account the fact that some of us may have limited access, or none at all, to certain of the senses, such as sight, we all nevertheless have some capacity to be sensual. Unfortunately, however, sensuality, like feelings, is often downplayed—it is regarded as less important than intellect or thinking.

For our purposes of exploration, I will not restrict the discussion to our capacities to see, hear, smell, taste or touch. Instead, let's look at the results of our ability to be sensual—in other words, how we either allow or disallow sensuality and how we rate ourselves as sensual women, how much we *believe in our interpretations of what we see, hear, smell, taste or touch.*

Sensuality vs. Sexuality

Before we go any further, let's clear up a possible confusion. Are *sensuality* and *sexuality* the same? The words have often been used interchangeably, perhaps even to the degree that we forget that they are indeed quite different. Certainly, advertising has contributed to the muddle. Use a particular product and you're immediately sensual. The accompanying picture looks sexual. Some advertisers may be afraid to say sexual. Perhaps they believe it's too blatant. That could be the reason why some women do not freely admit sensuality; they are afraid they will be unfavorably labeled as sexual.

But isn't this the age of "sexual freedom"? Surely sexual taboos exist now only in the minds of old ladies, mothers, aunts, grandmothers and fathers.

My experience with women of all ages in my therapy practice presents a great deal of evidence that contradicts any notion that women today are any more comfortable with their sexuality, or with "sexual freedom," than were women in the past who endured sexual restraint. Women remain confused about their sensuality and their sexuality.

Sensuality Quiz

Let's return to sensuality. In order to determine how much you allow yours, give yourself a little quiz.

1. Do you often observe your environment?
2. Are cacti sensual?

3. Is removing a splinter as sensual as touching silk?
4. Is your opinion about art or music as important as another's opinion?
5. Is Kansas as interesting as California?
6. Do you close your eyes when you are making love?
7. Have you ever watched an animal for a time and just wondered?
8. Do you allow yourself to explore your own body and enjoy the sensations?

Were your answers all yes, or all no, or half and half? Don't be concerned about your tally because there aren't any right answers. The questions were posed to allow you to understand the many different aspects of sensuality. Let's explore the questions, one at a time.

1. *Do you often observe your environment?* I live in the Rocky Mountains, and I observe my environment. But that's because I'm who I am—not because I live in the mountains. When I'm in Denver, I observe traffic, people, plays and art. In the mountains, I observe snow, people, aspen trees, alpenglow, snow tires and hummingbirds. What about where you live?

2. *Are cacti sensual?* Have you ever seen the desert in bloom? The flowers on cacti are extravagant and beautiful. But cacti have stickers. Well, so do roses—and grandmother's horsehair couch. Is a maple tree in autumn more beautiful than a cactus in bloom? What about the plant life where you are?

3. *Is removing a splinter as sensual as touching silk?* If you have ever removed a splinter from a child's finger, you know that the tensions and anxieties that you and the child experience approach those that accompany a

heart transplant. Splinters hurt—there's no doubt about it no matter what age you are. But silk is smooth and pliable—not like splinters. Silk is cool and beautiful. And why do some people love the feel of a fuzzy rug, especially in front of a fireplace—and especially when the fuzziness is directly on their naked skin? Have you ever stroked silk? Or removed a splinter and felt the pain? Or luxuriated in warmth?

4. *Is your opinion about art or music as important as another's opinion?* How often have you visited an art gallery with your friend and heard her or him comment on an art piece that you really liked? If the comment was positive, did you feel reinforced? If it was negative, did you wonder about your sensibilities and intelligence? Did you question the other person's? Have you ever attended a concert that you didn't like but everyone else did and thought you should have too? It could have been the local symphony, the New York Philharmonic or The Grateful Dead. Did you wonder, "What's wrong with me?" Can you remember when you expressed an opinion that was questioned in an authoritative manner by someone else? Did you then doubt yourself?

5. *Is Kansas as interesting as California?* It depends largely on where you live—especially if you live in either Kansas or California. Isn't that the real point? If you live in Ohio, isn't it important to appreciate Ohio, instead of longing to live in Maine? Every place has beauty, if only we allow our sensuality to help us appreciate the uniqueness. Are the loons in Canada more interesting than the roadrunners in New Mexico? Doesn't it depend on what you enjoy?

6. *Do you close your eyes when you are making love?* If you do, it could be for a variety of reasons. Let's suppose it's because you want to concentrate on the touch of your

lover's skin or the smell of his body or the sounds he is making. How do you feel when he is stroking you? Is this sensual or sexual? Or both? Can you permit yourself to fully succumb to your senses?

7. *Have you ever watched an animal for a time and just wondered?* Why do brown weasels turn into white ermines? How can one horse team pull three tons and another horse team pull a carriage in perfect synchronization? Have you ever tended a wounded animal? Or pointed out a nest to your children and explained its purpose? Why do you enjoy stroking your cat or dog? Have you watched an animal giving birth?

8. *Do you allow yourself to explore your own body and enjoy the sensations?* Or have you learned that stroking yourself is wrong? Do you avoid standing naked in front of a mirror or in front of your lover? Even though you recognize the relaxing quality of a long bubble bath, how often do you enjoy one? Have you ever sat in a Jacuzzi and, eyes closed, enjoyed the warm and bubbly water pulsating on your body? Do you limit yourself to using lotion on your face and hands and ignore the rest of your body? Consider how free you are to sensually enjoy your own body.

Sensuality, Feeling, Thinking and Behavior

When you reflect on the questions you've just asked yourself, you can see how sensuality, feelings, thinking and behavior are intertwined. Your thinking, often the result of what you have been taught, can definitely inhibit your sensuality—if you allow it. However, when you claim your individual right to be sensual and to value your interpretations of what you see, hear, smell, taste or touch, you will be claiming another very important part of yourself and taking a major step toward self-management and personal power—again, the keys to connecting and self-actualization.

If you are having any trouble doing that, ask yourself why. Is it because you have learned to undervalue your sensual reactions about life as you experience it? If you learned to value your abilities to be sensual and to trust your opinions, how would that affect your self-worth?

The women in the groups have had some interesting answers to that question.

"How you carry yourself as a person is passed to others. They become more aware of you when you're more aware of yourself: how you carry yourself, how you speak about the things that are important to you. The more sensual you become, the more people around you become aware of that."

"When you allow your sensuality, it's the way you truly are. It's not an act."

"Sensuality is self-assurance. If you know you can handle you and the way you are, then you have time to be aware of a lot of other things."

"When you experience yourself sensually, you're comfortable to experience so many new things."

"When you're comfortable with yourself, when you value your own sensuality, you don't have to be interacting with someone and getting feedback and endorsement of yourself. You just have it already, you're comfortable."

The women enjoyed the discussions about sensuality because most of them had never considered their sensual abilities to be a separate part of themselves, a part to be valued. They were able to realize that their sensuality is deeply entwined with all their feelings, thoughts and behaviors. Recognizing that to be important, they added another dimension to high self-worth. Most of the women had previously confused sensuality with sexuality. They all agreed that sensuality plays a major part in sexuality.

Sexuality

Without a doubt, allowing yourself to be fully sensual, and appreciating your sensuality, adds depth to your sexuality. Generally, little girls are cuddled, stroked, hugged, admired and touched. They learn to be comfortable with these sensual expressions of affection. As women they may transfer the sensual expressions of affection to sexuality and love behavior. Sensuality, sexuality and love can become a synergistic total. The three components achieve an effect greater than each is individually capable of achieving. In this triangle, sexual behavior is not considered as a separate entity. But even though women view sex as a part of love and intimacy, they may still have a lot of difficulty with their sexuality. "Free sex" or "more sex" or "sexual freedom" has not alleviated the difficulty, because the difficulty resides in a variety of early learnings.

Early Lessons

As we've already observed, a great many women do not accept their bodies. Not only have they learned nonacceptance because they compare themselves unfavorably with others, but they may also have learned that their bodies have a certain *vulgarity.*

That's right. Occasionally women have used that word. They are so self-loathing that they cannot stand the sight of their own genitals. Menstruation is "the curse" or they say they've "come sick." Many young girls thought they were bleeding to death when their first period started, and because it was never explained, it was interpreted as shameful or secretive.

Remember the films you were required to watch in the fourth or fifth or sixth grade? Perhaps your mother had to sign a permission slip, and the boys weren't allowed in; they had their own films and girls weren't allowed. Then we found out about intercourse and where babies came from. ("Well, maybe *your* folks did it, but certainly *mine* didn't!") However incredulous or embarrassed the children might be, these lessons are generally positive. It's only when a child learns that sexuality is not okay that the lessons are harmful. And sometimes these harmful lessons begin quite early.

When little boys are potty trained, they are encouraged to grasp their penises and aim correctly. Initially, they are usually rewarded for simply taking hold, no matter where they aim. Their skill improves and they are rewarded more. (No one really notices whether they *enjoy* holding their penises.) They are also taught in the bathtub to thoroughly clean the penis. (That probably feels good.) They are rewarded for cleanliness.

What about little girls? Well, they sit down. They don't need to aim. And if they put their hands down, except to quickly clean themselves, they may be reprimanded or have their hands slapped. Then they are taught to be modest. "Keep your dress down." "Keep your legs close together." "Watch how you sit." Undoubtedly, each of us has at least one story that is unique, and we all have many stories in common. The point is that both little girls and little boys frequently are not taught to appreciate their sexuality and how it fits in with the other components of their personalities.

Can you imagine how much easier your growing up

would have been if your parents had openly discussed with you the feelings, both emotional and physical, that you were experiencing? Do you think you might have been more comfortable and had less worry and concern about your sexuality if you had learned about the responsibilities that accompany sexual behavior—the responsibilities that include emotional and sexual interaction, the pain of rejection, the obligations of pregnancy?

Instead, many women were taught fear, guilt and shame instead of responsibility. It's no wonder that female sexuality is so often full of conflict.

One lesson that many of us women were strongly taught was that boys wanted sex; they needed sex and it was our job to keep them under control until we were married. Then we were supposed to know everything to do sexually (within limits, of course) to keep our marriages together, to keep our husbands from straying.

Initially, I thought that perhaps the lesson I just stated was learned only by women who are now forty or older, but numerous younger women have confirmed that they learned some version of the same lesson. The fact is that sexuality remains conflictive.

The irony in the lesson, of course, is that although we women are supposed to know a great deal about sexual behavior, we are taught very little. We're also supposed to be sexy in order to attract a man, but we must not be *sexual* until the appropriate time. I've observed, in a college setting, young women who were pregnant because they didn't use birth control. Why—in this day and age? Because they believed that to use birth control methods implied that they were *planning* to have intercourse. So rather than freely admit ahead of time the possibility of intercourse, they took a chance, using hope as the birth control method. That, by some twisted way of thinking, was more acceptable than planning.

Sex, Marriage and the Caught Caretaker

Women have also learned that good sex—good enough to keep your husband or lover interested in you only—is the woman's responsibility. If your man strays, it's your fault. If your man is impotent, it's your fault. If sex is unsatisfactory, it's your fault. If you don't experience orgasm, it's your fault. If your partner's technique is bad, it's your fault. If you become pregnant, it's your fault. These stereotypical messages fit right into the framework of the caught caretaker. She is in charge, and being caught, she will unquestionably buy into the power; she sees it as her responsibility. If the sex or relationship or marriage doesn't work well, it's her fault.

The caught caretaker will not allow herself to challenge any of these stereotypical messages, because her fears of loss are too great. However, by trying to remain in charge, because it's her duty, she doubles her risk of losing. She cannot allow the man to assume responsibility for himself or one-half the responsibility for the relationship. If she did, she would be out of a job.

And what are her feelings? Well, let us hope that there is *love*. Being a caught caretaker does not negate the possibility of loving. Love is very important. But that love has a slim chance for survival in the face of the caught caretaker's guilt, shame and fear. And when she fails, as she sees it, she's angry but unable to acknowledge it.

If a woman does finally recognize that she is responsible for herself as well as to the relationship, and that her mate has the same responsibilities, she will be well on her way to assertive freedom. She won't be caught. Assertive freedom is wonderfully freeing, but in order to achieve it, women will want to give up some old behaviors.

Using sex as an indirect and dishonest communication tool is one such behavior. Quite frankly, rewarding your lover with sex, granting sex as a gift or withholding sex are ways to try to gain control. Withholding sex instead of directly acknowledging your feelings, usually anger, is punishment. Awarding sex is the pay-off, the reward your lover receives for his good behavior.

Another dishonest behavior to give up is faking pleasure or orgasm. A caught caretaker may fake because she believes it's her responsibility to make sure her lover believes that he is adequate. He must not feel bad about his abilities. However, trying to make sure her man feels sexually powerful is not the only reason women fake orgasm and pleasure. Another major reason is that by faking pleasure a woman presents herself as a sexually responsive woman, a woman who is just as sexually responsive, maybe even more so, than any other woman. In other words, she fakes to compete.

Yet another old behavior to abandon is focusing on your partner's experience instead of your own. That fits right in with the caught caretaker. Of course it's important to pay attention to your partner's pleasure, but not at the cost of yours. You and your partner are equal participants in sexual intimacy, and that equality is vital. Without it, your relationship will eventually become boring and unrewarding; it will falter and die.

Many women continue to respond to the question, "What is the most important female sex organ?" by answering, "The vagina." This reply illustrates the emphasis on male pleasure. The focus on *his* pleasure exclusively feeds *her* martyrdom. Her passivity becomes her trap and turns into aggressiveness. Then she will use sex as a manipulation tool, and the intimacy she so desires will be beyond realization.

The good news is that there is recent evidence that women have begun to recognize the importance of asserting their interest in their own sexual satisfaction in addition to that of their partners. For example, women have begun to answer that the brain, the clitoris or the skin is the most important female sex organ.

In addition, there is literature abundantly available that emphasizes the importance of mutual satisfaction and assertive behavior in sex. It becomes very important that a woman take direct responsibility for her sexuality, her pleasure and her gratification. Without doing so, she will reinforce the old myth that men are sexual exploiters, and she will feel used and angry.

She will also be likely to believe the myth that men know all there is to know about sex, again setting the stage for frustration and disappointment. Men have suffered their versions of misguided and embarrassed sexual teachings as much as women.

Generally speaking—prior to the pill, live-in arrangements, acceptance of divorce and single motherhood—couples got married in order to have sex legally and without guilt and fear. There's no debating that sex in a marriage is extremely important. As a matter of fact, sex is one of the first things to suffer when a relationship is in trouble. But getting married in order to have sex is very dangerous. It's imperative that there be many other important reasons why a couple chooses to marry. Sexual activity carries a weight of accountabilities that must be observed. Acceptance of this fact by both partners is a big plus for a lasting relationship.

Men and Sexuality

An interesting aspect in the area of sexual understanding has been my discovery, in the course of therapy interviews, that men are often extremely frightened of sexual interactions. Despite all the lessons taught to women that they are responsible for sex, men are still the performers, and "sexual freedom" has encouraged performance anxiety. For example, learning about a woman's capacity for multiple orgasms can cause a man to worry about his ability to meet his partner's needs.

As you begin to explore your own learnings, beliefs and myths about your sexuality, remind yourself that men have their own hang-ups. Men are taught to be goal-oriented. Sexual conquest is a measure of masculinity. While little girls are held and cuddled and hugged and stroked, little boys are taught to compete and conquer.

Sometimes men also are ill prepared for a sexually assertive woman—something they may have thought they wanted. They may feel overwhelmed and threatened. If that is the case, they may try their own form of manipulation through labeling: aggressive, nonfeminine, pushy. Or they may start inhibiting their own sexual assertiveness because they fear more of a response than they believe they can handle.

The concerns can become very complicated, and they go both ways in a relationship. But only a caught caretaker believes sexual dissatisfaction is her fault exclusively.

Obstacles to Sexuality

So-called "sexual freedom" may have many good points, but sometimes they are hard to find. In addition, "sexual freedom" has dangerous pitfalls for a woman who lacks self-confidence. What kinds of things do we allow to interfere with our sexuality?

1. *A poor body image.* This is an extremely complex concern. If you regard yourself as physically nonacceptable, or use obesity to disguise a discomfort with sex, or become anorexic to be acceptable, you have serious psychological and physical problems to confront. But you don't have to go to these extremes in order to allow a poor body image to interfere with your sexuality.

2. *Fatigue.* Work is highly valued in our society. You may try to do too much in a short period of time. You may be a caught caretaker who is trying out for a superwoman role. Also, constantly feeling guilt, fear and shame is very tiring. So is trying to disguise anger. Working in order to delay going to bed so that you can avoid your partner's advances may look acceptable, but not for long. Eventually it's hard to disguise your discomfort and nonassertiveness.

3. *Shoulds.* This obstacle may seem a little less complex, but only on the surface. You can examine your shoulds, as you did in Chapter 5, to see whether they are relevant for you now. But then you will encounter those well-learned feelings. You can help yourself by using the five steps to change outlined in Chapter 4.

4. *Anger.* You can't enjoy lovemaking if you're angry (although it sometimes appears that men have that capacity). In *Sexual Joy,* Michael and Dorothy Clarke identify the "twenty-three-and-a-half-hour foreplay":

> A woman is more likely to be stirred to sexual arousal if she has slept well and has had a good day, if there were no harsh words at breakfast, and her job or her children have left her free of frustration

or fatigue. The evening has been relaxing, not necessarily filled with conversation, but there has been an awareness of doing things together— watching television perhaps, or reading a book— but in the same room, aware of each other's presence. Bedtime lovemaking then comes as a pleasing opportunity to express good feelings that have been steadily mounting all day. [1]

The twenty-three-and-a-half-hour foreplay scenario can certainly have many different settings and circumstances. The important element is to feel relaxed, comfortable and loved. You cannot achieve those feelings if you have not handled any anger you might have experienced. Anger does not necessarily preclude the twenty-three-and-a-half-hour foreplay. Handling anger so that you avoid resentment is being self-managing, and claiming personal power will enhance your desire to be together with your partner.

5. *Nonassertiveness.* Believing that you do not have personal rights is very inhibiting. That's a simple statement with far-reaching results. Refer to Chapter 7 and you will easily understand how passivity inhibits sensuality and sexuality. The other extreme—aggression—is equally inhibiting, of course.

6. *Confusion about expectations.* If you believe that the sexual activity described in popular romantic movies and letters to *Playboy* is the way it should be, you are in trouble. You will surely be inhibited with guilt and shame that you don't always experience simultaneous, tumultuous climax—or that you don't climax at all. You will fear that your sexual interest won't match your partner's interest in frequency or coincidence of mutual desire.

7. *Age myths.* At a medical seminar, I remember hearing that a male's sexual power peaks at age nineteen and goes downhill from then on. Women, however, are likely to encounter their peak years between thirty and fifty. Furthermore, there appears to be increasing evidence that sexual interest after menopause is much greater than had formerly been accepted or understood.

If these are facts, then what occurs that causes a woman to feel inhibited by her age? The answer is that women—and men—have been programmed to believe that when a woman grows older, she becomes less attractive and, therefore, less desirable.

8. *Fear of rejection, betrayal or abandonment.* If a woman has experienced such losses, allowing herself to become vulnerable again will be difficult. The fears are intense, and the memories of the feelings that accompany rejection, betrayal and abandonment are reminders to go easy with any new relationships.

Sometimes we allow ourselves to enter experimental stages after loss. These experiments can be painful when we are full of self-doubts, but they can, at the same time, be helpful to us to learn new wisdoms in an ever-changing society.

9. *Using sex as an indirect communication.* Refer to the earlier discussion in this chapter, "Sex, Marriage and the Caught Caretaker."

10. *The feelings of being unlovable, undeserving or unworthy.* A woman who believes herself to be unlovable, undeserving or unworthy, who still carries poor self-worth messages from the past, may use sexual behavior as an attempt to achieve intimacy and the feelings of being lovable and desirable. For example, dressing in a sexually provocative style will probably gain the attention of

men. The woman may present herself as sexually available but actually be very afraid of sexual interaction because the goal is to gain attention, not action. On the other hand, a woman with negative self-love may welcome the advancements of men, becoming promiscuous in her attempts to feel loved. But one man's love could never be enough to prove to her her own worthiness, so she becomes indiscriminately sexually active, a behavior that continually reinforces her low self-esteem.

Or, a woman who suffers from these feelings may totally reject herself as a sexual person and live a life of loneliness and isolation. She might fall prey to the caught caretaker role or devote herself to professional achievements—she will do whatever she can to avoid attracting attention to herself. The fear of intimacy rules her life.

The gray area between these two extremes is where most women who submit to these low self-worth messages will be leading their lives. If the feeling of being unlovable, undeserving or unworthy is your message from the past, challenge it. Don't work hard to prove that your message is correct. It has no relevancy for you in the present.

Sexual Inhibitions

There are no easy answers. The sex manuals or pop sex instruction books rarely address psychological reasons for inhibitions. They prey on false hopes that employing successive back rubs and assuming new positions will solve any problems we encounter. We're to allow fantasies, and by fantasizing, we are supposed to be able to enjoy unlimited pleasure. Back rubs, fantasies, new positions and sexy lingerie can be helpful, but they aren't the solutions.

Sometimes women are instructed to "let go." Of what? If inhibitions could be released simply on the instruction to "let go," change would be easy and resolutions simple. Our learnings are too complex to just "let go." At the same time that we're taught to be responsible for good sex, we also learn that we aren't supposed to be "sexy," except in certain circumstances. We learn to feel shame and guilt because we're taught fear instead of accountability.

We're taught caretaking to such an extent that if there is a concern, it is undoubtedly our fault, and we look for problems within ourselves instead of considering that perhaps our partners have the problem, or at least a part of it.

Sexual Freedom

You may have noticed that, in this chapter, I have often enclosed the term "sexual freedom" in quotation marks. That's because I'm not sure what it really means. It appears to connote a variety of ideas: living together; easy sex; frequent, enjoyable, demanding sex; more explicit sex in books, movies and on TV. These connotations do not convince me that "sexual freedom" is freedom at all.

The only way to achieve real "sexual freedom" is to understand yourself and then put your self-management skills to work. When you are able to comprehend your behaviors, you can choose those that fit easily into your own moral and social values. You can learn to trust yourself and act on your own intuitions. Decide what values are important to you and don't press the limits too much, or you might put yourself in a constant agony of questioning that leads to feelings of guilt and consequent low self-worth. Remember that as you challenge yourself, you may feel some anxiety. This is a natural result of change. As you challenge your old, conditioned learnings, you may not discover any easy answers to replace them.

Initial attempts to become more assertive by openly claiming your sexuality may seem threatening to you and your partner. However, this is the pathway to focusing on the total relationship. Sexual intimacy will be only a symbol of the quality of your relationship and not the end result.

A really wonderful thing about sexual connecting is that you *feel* it, both emotionally and physically. The physical feelings are encompassing: you have physical reactions. Appreciating your sensuality and expressing your sexuality are enhancements. You feel nurturing, caring, loving, understanding and accepting. You can express your connecting feelings in a variety of ways that range from the very assertive statement "I love you" and sexual intercourse, to "I love you" and a hug, to "I care" and a smile, to "I accept" and a handshake.

The opportunity to enjoy your sensuality and your sexuality will become your reality when you understand and accept yourself, when you free yourself from guilt, shame, fear and anger. Then you will be open to connecting and self-actualization.

Notes

1. Michael and Dorothy Clarke, *Sexual Joy* (Sydney, Australia: Pan Books, 1989), pp. 84–85. Reprinted with permission.

11
. . . .
Communication

This book has been liberally peppered with refer-
ences to high self-worth or high self-esteem,
awareness and personal power. By now, I'm
sure you can appreciate the importance I ascribe to
these concepts and their accompanying feelings,
thoughts and behavior. In addition, I'm sure you also
have your own interpretations and insights.

How can you communicate your interpretations of
these concepts? Your personal style is crucial. Do you
believe yourself to be an effective communicator? Or
are you experiencing some difficulty? What is happening when you are "on the same wavelength" as someone? What is missing when you "just aren't communicating"?

What Is Communication?

Communication is a tool that allows us to function in the world. It is the measurement of our interactions with one another, our achievements, the quality of our lives. In *Peoplemaking*, Virginia Satir emphasizes that each of us is born with no self-concept, no knowledge of interactions and no experience.[1] These things are developed from hour one by our communication with others.

She also points out that each of us has certain common elements of communication, through which all communication occurs. These are:

1. Our bodies—the way we look and the ways we move.
2. Our senses—seeing, hearing, smelling, tasting and touching.
3. Our values—the guidelines by which we have chosen to live.
4. Our expectations—the beliefs we have formed from past experiences.
5. Our brains—the interpreters of our experiences.
6. Our ability to talk—our voices and our hands, our language.

When you review the list you will quickly notice that even though the elements of communication are common to us all, each element is personally unique. Therein lies an important fundamental for effective communication: *recognizing the uniqueness of each element for each person regardless of age or sex.*

How Do We Communicate?

When you attempt to communicate, you bring all of the elements into play. Before you speak, you experience an internal activity.

Immediately you notice how the other person looks. You do this through your senses. Then your brain interprets this information, using your values and your expectations. The other person is doing exactly the same thing. All of this happens before you talk to each other, and generally without a lot of conscious thought.

When you are "on the same wavelength," you will have similar common elements. You will be pleasing to each other physically. You will enjoy what you see and hear. You will take pleasure in the way she or he shakes your hand or smiles at you. Your values, influenced by your personal reflections and decisions, will be compatible even though your backgrounds may be different. Your expectations will be relative because they will have been formed by similar coping styles. It will be easy and comfortable to talk.

What happens when you "just aren't communicating"? The common elements are still there, and even though they are common, they are different. Your impressions, interpreted by your senses, values and expectations, aren't positive. You don't like what you see. You may be rejecting, because the way the other person looks, smells and sounds elicits adverse reactions, based on your values. Your past experiences will tell you not to expect any meaningful dialogue. What you say may be provocative or defensive. You may believe it's too dangerous to be open or sharing. But "just not communicating" can be changed to "the same wavelength" if you want that to happen.

"We don't communicate" is used more than any

other statement to sum up the problems of relationships, both personal and professional. The statement seems to indicate that if people could just learn to communicate effectively, their problems would be solved. While that assumption is simplistic, it is true that people don't communicate their honest thoughts and feelings, so that relationships shatter, or at least reach the breaking point, jobs are lost and connecting is interrupted. Good communication is a vital tool for effective functioning and self-management.

Why Is Communication Difficult?

So why do people have so much difficulty saying what they mean and meaning what they say? Sometimes people will answer, "We don't know *how* to communicate." Again, that's often very true. The skills of effectively communicating appear to be poorly learned, but they can be mastered. We can learn how to say what we want to say and also how to listen in a complimentary fashion to the speaker.

Obstacles to Communication

Even with the skills, people often do not communicate effectively. Why?

Principally because of fear. People are afraid to communicate to others what they are really feeling and thinking. Stop for a minute to reflect. What really stops you from saying what you want to say? Very often, it is fear of the response. Others won't like what we say or they will think we sound dumb or off-base or silly. We're fearful of the opinion, so we don't say anything at all. We don't want to be judged an intellectual clod.

We may also be fearful of an aggressive response. If anger is difficult for us to handle, we will avoid saying anything we believe may evoke an aggressive reply. If we are feeling angry, we might be so unaccepting of the feeling that we avoid any expression. We may also be fearful that an argument will ensue, or even fighting or physical abuse. So we keep quiet, even when our feeling of anger increases.

We may be fearful that if we say what we want to say, the listener will feel hurt or criticized. So we say nothing, yet we're left with our own feelings of discomfort or disapproval. Connecting lines are broken.

Further blocks may reside in our fears about intimacy and commitment. We don't want to reveal too much about ourselves; others may use it against us, talk about us or reject us.

If we keep ourselves to ourselves, we believe we won't suffer any loss of self through revelations to another. Our myth is that being guarded is safe. While remaining silent or allowing only polite interchange will guard against any possible commitment, such a choice also guards against connecting. What we are trying to do is guard ourselves from rejection or loss.

Feeling fearful is the primary block to successful communication. We may say we don't know *how* to communicate, but, although it may be true that our skills could be enhanced, our fears are the real barriers.

Recognizing that truth, how can we handle the fears? The answers aren't easy, of course, because our fears are usually based in our realities. We may have actually experienced rejection, criticism or another's aggression or abuse. We may have felt responsible for another's feeling hurt or criticized if we believed we caused their reactions. Our own defenses, necessary for us, may inhibit us from revealing too much; we can't risk being vulnerable.

Do you recall from Chapter 3 your message from the past? Using Laura and her husband's situation as a model, can you see the system that operates in the relationship? Her perception of criticism leads to aggressiveness—leads to his perception of control—leads to withdrawal—leads to perceived rejection (What's wrong with you?)—leads to aggressiveness—leads to . . . on and on. When Laura and her husband get into this system, all effective communication stops. The system takes over.

Think about your message. Can you see any systems that are operating between you and those with whom you want to communicate? There are always systems in any relationship and they may be difficult to comprehend. In some cases, a third party or a counselor may be able to assist with a more objective point of view. Comprehending your systems, one of the most important tools for handling your fears, can open the door to productive communication.

When you recognize that fear is an allowable feeling for women, you can understand why women have a lot of trouble confronting their own fears. When we're fearful, we're considered passive and feminine. In many ways, society rewards women for being poor communicators by labeling us as thoughtful and considerate. We certainly aren't challenging. We appear to be ever mindful of how someone else will react. At first glance, our fears can look like caretaking.

It's always good to dig a little deeper, to develop awareness so you can handle any fears, using your high self-esteem. If you don't do that task, you will risk an important threat to your communicating effectively, and to the connecting and self-actualization that result from that contact. Let's explore a few other obstacles to effective communication.

When you were in elementary school, did you learn to diagram sentences? Sentence diagramming helps you identify parts of speech as you place the words of a sentence in certain areas on the diagram. There is no room for creativity—every word has its place; the structure is rigid.

In our lives, we often use phrases that are analogous to, "Every word has its place." A few are: "I've got all my ducks in a row," "Everything is decided," "Don't try to fit square pegs into round holes," "It's all settled," and, especially, "I'm right."

Of course, "I'm right" means "You're wrong." When this type of reasoning occurs, there is only right or wrong, fair or unfair, just or unjust, correct or incorrect, logical or illogical, true or false, positive or negative, win or lose. The view of life is black or white.

This is hardly self-actualizing because a self-actualized person understands that there are many shades of gray between black and white. Statements or beliefs that represent thinking in terms of logical, true, right or any of the other extremes are based in a rigidity that will severely restrict communication.

Because our beliefs and opinions are formed by our own experiences, each of us has a separate point of view. Our view may agree with another's, but it may also be diametrically opposed. When we defend our opinions, beliefs or perceptions strongly, indicating that they are logical or right or the only way to view the matter, what happens? Often arguments ensue.

As you know, when there are arguments, people end up as alienated opponents, defending their viewpoints as if they were engraved in stone. This type of activity reflects a lack of understanding that each person has individual beliefs, opinions and perceptions. It can also indicate that one hasn't determined for oneself how to live life in a self-actualized fashion by making choices that are personally meaningful and fulfilling. There is a strong tendency to follow predefined and unquestioned shoulds and rules, to follow the diagram's rigid structure. There is little, if any, willingness to consider another point of view. "Rules are rules and that's the way it *should* be."

When you rigidly stick to rules or shoulds that you have not determined through your own exploration to be what you want, you risk giving away, by default, your chance to decide for yourself, to form your own opinions and beliefs. If you have seriously questioned yourself, it's likely that you comprehend that there are many different options, opinions, understandings and beliefs. What is right for you may be wrong for someone else.

But it is also extremely difficult for us to be objective about ourselves. When you accept this fact, your chances for effective communication will greatly increase because you will be seeking answers for your behavior and feelings and thoughts within yourself. Ask yourself why instead of insisting upon another's why.

Once in a while, a couple will come in for counseling, and the message clearly given by one partner is that "if only she (he) would change, I would be okay." The task for this couple is very difficult, to say the least, and unless there is a change in the rigid attitude, the chance for reconciliation and communication is nil.

Yet, sometimes a very interesting thing follows. The person who so rigidly believes that he or she is right or correct is always the loser if the other partner chooses to examine his or her own personal dynamics. Frequently the self-examiner is the woman, indicating her strong desire for awareness and self-management. My faith in women's strengths has been greatly increased because of this phenomenon.

Unclear Messages

Another block to effective communication is that often people aren't speaking the same language. That is, one person uses the language of feeling and the other uses the language of thinking. As you learned earlier, each of us has the capacity for being both a feeling person and a thinking person. Unless two people are responding to each other by recognizing that there is both feeling-motivated speaking and thinking-motivated speaking, disagreements and arguments may occur.

For example, consider these two people: one the parent, Katy, and one the stepparent, Don, who are talking about Katy's child, who has exhibited a behavior that neither she nor Don likes. Katy has started the discussion and related the behavior. Don listens and then agrees that the behavior of the child is unacceptable, perhaps adding words that indicate the impracticality, insensibility, absurdity or stupidity of the behavior. Then he goes on to make suggestions about how Katy could have handled or could now handle the situation.

At this point, there's a good possibility Katy and Don will begin to speak different languages. Katy may have more *feeling* about the child and the behavior than Don. Katy can be in full agreement with all of Don's logical (thinking) statements and suggestions, but because she has feelings about her child that could range from guilt to shame to fear to anger, underscored by love, she has shifted to feelings, while Don has remained in a thinking mode.

Katy, in this example, could interpret Don's thinking-motivated language as nonsupport and feel criticized. Despite an intellectual understanding between the partners, a disagreement could flare.

Another example: Jason and Sue are discussing the possibility of a move to another city. Jason is very excited (a feeling) but Sue is very anxious (a feeling). While the move means a job promotion and raise for him, the move means a job loss for her. He points out (a shift to thinking) that she won't have to work at all, accompanying his statements with examples of how wonderful it will be for her. She can understand, but she is still feeling fear and loss. He just can't understand what's wrong with her; she's being irrational.

In the two examples, both people have some thinking and some feeling. The person who is mostly thinking becomes very rational, and the person who is mostly feeling becomes very emotional and is labeled irrational. The thinking person is dumbfounded that the feeling person can't see the logic of the situation. Then there may be a heated exchange that ends in an impasse. The feeling person may feel very frustrated and inadequate, because in our society, practicality and rationality are highly valued.

When you recognize that there are the two types of sublanguages, you can begin to watch for them. It's useless to try to talk thinking to a person who is feeling. The feelings must be handled before any logic can be heard. This can be accomplished by asking, "What are you feeling?" It will probably be fear, frustration, anger, anxiety, loss, disappointment, guilt or love—or all of the above. When you say that you understand and support the feelings, then you can both talk thinking and move to solutions.

In addition to fear, rigidity and speaking two different languages, there's also the problem of definition.

One day I was listening to two people talk about being naive. As they went on with the conversation, I began to think that they were talking about two different things. So I asked what they meant when they used the word. The man answered that *naive* meant being inexperienced in business. The woman, looking astounded at the reply, answered that *naive* meant being inexperienced in sex. While they both understood naive as inexperience, they were using the same word to define dramatically different concepts.

All of us have a tendency to do the same thing. Because we comprehend out of our own values, experiences and expectations, we each have unique definitions for certain words. Some of these important personalized words are: *love, commitment, everlasting, beautiful, ugly, angry, correct, fair, happiness, best, normal, inadequate, dependent, generous, rich, faithful, tired, fantastic, overworked, eligible, cruel.* These words, only a few examples, have dictionary definitions, but we also have our own, based on our individual experience, values and expectations. For this reason, it's vital that two people who are trying to achieve effective communication understand as clearly as possible what the other means when she or he uses qualitative words.

Sometimes it doesn't really matter so much in casual conversations, but just imagine what kind of confusion and misunderstanding could occur if one person defines commitment as loving another all one's life, focusing constant attention on the loved one, and the other person defines commitment as attempting to make the relationship work. Even if the two people love each other and really want to communicate, there is a strong possibility of disagreement because they are using the same word to describe different beliefs, behaviors and feelings.

Once you recognize that this type of problem occurs, you can address the solution easily. I'm certainly not suggesting that when your lover says, "I love you," that you interrupt and ask, "Just what do you mean by *love?*" But you can select opportunities for discussing interpretations of words that you and an important other person may be defining quite differently. Think about the qualitative words you use, and write down your definitions. Many people have not bothered to clearly identify their own meanings. They just think it should be clear, especially to someone who loves them, even when they aren't clear themselves. Then ask your partner to do the same thing. Then, accept each other's definition. You will be able to do this by reminding yourself that each of us, while sharing the common elements of communication, has unique personal experiences, expectations and values that contribute to our separate definitions.

A close cousin to the problem of definition is the problem of interpretation of the statements. Do you remember the story in Chapter 9 of the woman who had grown up with a lot of criticisms and who responded to my question, "Where did you get that blouse?" with "What's the matter? Don't you like it?" Her interpretation came from the criticism in her past. Because each of us has a past, we tend to filter events and communications through our own cheesecloth of experience. This may have something to do with your message from the past. You can use your self-awareness to interrupt this block.

Another barrier to effective communication is that

often we don't understand what another person is *meaning* to say. There are three principal reasons for the misunderstanding.

One is that we aren't fully listening. We're too busy trying to figure out what we will say next in order to appear intelligent, perceptive or witty, or to defend ourselves. When we do that, we often say something irrelevant, indicating that we haven't really heard what the speaker is saying. We may as well have a conversation with ourselves. If you are aggressively intent upon defending your position or your opinion, you will close the door for a discussion and open the door for an argument.

The second reason we often don't understand what the speaker is saying is that we translate the speaker's words in light of our own accounts of past interactions. Our expectations do not allow the possibility that the other person has changed, or has changed his or her thinking. We assume it will be the same old thing. Consequently, we again close the door for effective communication.

Third, it's important that the speaker say as clearly and concisely as possible what she or he intends. Then the speaker can ask, "What did you hear me say?" A good listener, an assertive listener, will try to understand the intentions of the speaker. The listener can reply, "I heard you say . . .," putting the speaker's message into his or her own words. Then the speaker can say, "Yes, that is what I meant" or "No, let me try again." Although this technique, the state-repeat-confirm method, may seem ponderous, it is a very good way to clarify your message. Listening is not a passive activity, as you learned in the chapter on assertiveness. Listening carefully and fully and accurately is as much an assertive skill as speaking clearly and to the point. It's a fifty-fifty deal.

Communication Patterns

Admittedly though, no matter how well you listen or ask questions, you won't get a clear message if the speaker's style is manipulative. Because the manipulator believes herself or himself to be powerless, the message will be indirect, unclear and designed to incite fear, guilt or shame, so that the listener will respond "correctly" by doing or saying what the manipulator desires. The receiver or listener, if unaware of this style, will eventually respond with anger. It may take a while, but the anger will occur and the relationship will weaken, perhaps even break.

The solution, of course, is to trust yourself enough so that you learn to speak assertively. The more you do this, the stronger you will feel. You will be utilizing your self-management skills so that you will no longer be manipulative or allow yourself to be manipulated. However, manipulation is such a common communication pattern in our society that we often don't realize we are manipulating or being manipulated until the uncomfortable feelings give us that feedback.

You can be on the alert for the behavior. As soon as someone says something similar to, "I'm going to be sick if you don't . . ." or "I won't love you if you . . ." or "Oh, nothing" when you've asked, "What's the matter?," you can catch the pattern immediately if you are aware of your feeling reactions.

Manipulation can be a very complex behavior, but there is one commonly used idiom that is manipulative. Whenever you ask a question and don't really want an answer, you are being manipulative. Ask a child, "Why did you leave your room in such a mess?" and you'll probably get an answer that you don't want to hear. What you really meant was, "Don't leave your room in such a mess" or "I want you to clean your room." You can certainly learn to be assertive so that you are using direct, honest and sincere language. But what about others? How can you counter manipulation?

First and foremost, do not allow yourself to succumb to your feelings of guilt, shame or fear. Remind yourself that you have self-management choices.

Second, be as aware as possible of how you define yourself. This is important, because if it is a positive self-definition, you will not respond with the feelings of guilt, shame or fear when you are accused or criticized. For example, if you pride yourself because you see yourself as empathetic and nurturing and outgoing, although you won't like being labeled "selfish," you won't rush to prove the manipulator incorrect if you are truly self-assured and confident. You can simply say, "I don't agree."

You will also be on the alert for manipulative compliments. A simple "thank you" will help to interrupt any attempted manipulation. Sometimes it's very difficult to separate sincere compliments from manipulative compliments. If you find yourself rushing to return a compliment, check your caretaker to see if you are caught and believe you *must* answer a compliment with a compliment.

A third technique is to answer manipulative questions with another question. Manipulator: "Why aren't you working on the charity project?" You: "Why do you ask?"

Another way to respond to manipulative questions is with a simple yes or no. Manipulator: "Have you signed up to work at the bazaar?" You: "No."

This technique may sound abrupt and rude, and indeed it can be. It is necessary for you to determine the circumstances. You have the option to add an explanation (instead of a justification). In this case, you will be answering a question assuming that the questioner wants information. This also counters manipulation.

A fourth way to interrupt manipulation is to believe what the manipulator is saying. For example, suppose a co-worker looks sad. You ask: "What's the matter? You look sad." The answer: "Nothing." You reply, "Oh, good," and you continue as if everything is okay. The manipulator is stuck with the manipulation.

A fifth counter-manipulative technique is to ask a question to verify the manipulator's statement. Manipulator: "This place is a mess. It's always a mess!" You: "Do you mean that you want me to clean it?"

Finally, but very importantly, be on the alert for manipulation through health issues, weakness or helplessness. A caught caretaker is especially vulnerable to these forms, because they are frequently expressed as *needs* that someone else—you—should handle, or at least relieve.

These techniques are simple, but they will give you a good start to allow effective communication. You will be teaching yourself self-awareness, assertion and self-management.

Another block to effective communication is to believe in the myth that someone who knows us very well, or loves us, will know what we want or how we feel. We don't need to say it, and if they miss it, it's their fault. If they loved us, they would just *know*! Well, if we were all capable of mind reading, we wouldn't need to talk at all. This block—believing the myth—probably disguises an unwillingness (fear, again) to say what you want or believe or feel; you want someone else to guess (correctly, of course).

Sometimes another person *will* guess correctly, especially if he or she knows you pretty well, but there's no guarantee. If it doesn't happen, then how do you feel? Unloved, misunderstood, disappointed, frustrated, hurt, upset? If you buy into this myth, you probably don't allow anger. It's much too direct.

Similar to mind reading is hinting. Hint: "I guess your new home must be lovely." Really meant: "I would like to see your home." Hint: "Everybody will be with friends on Thanksgiving," said with a sad look. Really meant: "I would like to be with friends (you)." A major reason we hint is that we perceive hinting to be safe from rejection or loss. It doesn't work. If the hint isn't taken, the feelings of rejection and loss are still there.

The first cousin to both mind reading and hinting is assuming, mentioned earlier in this chapter. We just assume something has been done because *we* would have done it. Or we assume our partners (or parents or bosses or children) will respond in a certain way because they have always responded that way.

Do you recall my mentioning that some people look angry when they are fearful? If you just assume they are angry, you might choose to avoid them when reinforcement and comfort are actually what they want. Assumptions are a direct block to changing. When a couple involved in marital therapy is trying new behaviors, it is vitally important that each partner give the other trust, respect and patience. That's the only way change will occur. If, instead, they hang on to the assumption that their partner's behavior will remain the same, they are unable to give the valuable outside feedback that reinforces change.

Take the risk to be assertive and direct. Ask questions when you want information. Volunteer information when you want your messages to be absolutely clear.

Two extremely important phrases are: "What do you want me to do?" and "I would like you to . . . ."

Another stumbling block to effective communication, especially in close relationships, is that we don't understand the symbols of love. What are symbols of love? They represent the ways each of us feels (receives) and expresses love and appreciation. The characteristics of our symbols originate in our past. The way love was expressed in our family is the primary basis.

In my couples' weekend retreat, an exercise identifying symbols of love for each partner produced a great deal of meaningful information. Each participant was asked to make two lists. At the top of one, the heading was "If you loved me, you would . . . ." The heading for the second was "Because I love you, I will . . . ." Here are some samples of the ways the leading statements were completed:

> If you loved me, you would . . .
>> share the housework.
>> hold me quietly when I'm tired.
>> let me watch football in peace.
>> spend more time with me.
>> play with the children.
>> be more careful with money.
>> take care of my car.
>> let me spout off without taking it
>> personally.

Because I love you, I will . . .
                cook your favorite foods.
                be interested in your work.
                ask, "How was your day?"
                be complimentary.
                watch you play softball.
                be ready to make love when you are.
                remember important dates.
                be cheerful.

Look at the two lists. You can quickly see that they are interchangeable. The way we love is the way we want to be loved. Understanding your own and others' symbols of love is very important for effective communication.

As you've seen throughout this book, the ways a caught caretaker has learned to express love—with duties, suppression of anger, indirectness, powerlessness—are actually detrimental to connecting. A caught caretaker does something else that interferes with connecting and effective communication. She concludes that if someone else is silent, looks sad, annoyed or angry or behaves or talks in such a way that expresses those feelings, it's *her* fault. Believing that she must be nurturing, caring, etc., to all people all the time, the caught caretaker will believe herself to be essential to another's functioning.

This myth is a real snare for her and her caretakee(s).

You can see how it works. The caught caretaker, concluding that it's her fault, rushes in to make it right, at the very least emotionally, because she feels fear that somehow she has failed. Then she may try to make it right or better by attempting to take control of the situation. In doing this, she may ignore the importance of supporting another person's feelings.

Because a caught caretaker is also manipulative, she won't ask direct questions that could clear the way for effective communication. Instead, she will try to mind-read, always keeping herself central to the solution.

Then she may insist that something must be the matter, or else the other person wouldn't be silent or look sad, etc. It's her task to fix it, and she will probably insist upon fixing it her way. If the other person rejects her "help," she will become angry—although she can't admit anger, either. She is really caught, but so is the other person. His or her autonomy is denied. The self-management tools are undermined so that dependency is encouraged.

A person who is caught in her caretaker role is not an effective communicator. There may be a few brief effective episodes, but essentially the communication will be antagonistic, indirect and strained. Challenging old, inefficient patterns, although difficult, is extremely rewarding.

Follow the five steps for change. Be sure to reward yourself repeatedly, because change is frequently not welcomed by a partner or others, because they always have some stake in keeping the old game (interaction) the way it is. Whenever I am encouraging people to examine and try new options, I warn that when they attempt to change the game (interaction) rules, usually the other player(s) will try to play the old game harder. It may appear that what you are attempting isn't working. But be consistent and patient. Change takes time.

The last communication barrier I want to emphasize, before listing the communication techniques, is our common tendency through our everyday language to assign responsibility to others.

We say, "You made me . . .," "I got talked into . . .," "I got hooked," "He forced me to. . .," plus a variety of other phrases. These are roughly equivalent to comedian Flip Wilson's "The devil made me do it." These phrases imply that we are helpless victims. They imply a powerlessness. Using "I" language is one of the most simple, yet significant, behaviors you can use to claim your personal power.

Some people, including me, learned that to start a sentence or written paragraph with "I" was indicative of self-concern and a lack of interest in others. To this day, I feel a little bit uncomfortable when I say, "I think (want, believe, feel, etc.)." At the same time, I know the necessity of using "I" when I'm trying to communicate to another something that I believe is important, perhaps an uncomfortable feeling I might have. For example: "I'm angry because . . . ."

Picture yourself in a tense discussion. Imagine the other person saying to you, "You made me mad" or "You shouldn't have done what you did" or "You're wrong." What's your feeling reaction? Do you feel defensive, perhaps criticized or attacked? Would you want to say something back that would be accusing, or make an attempt to set matters straight?

Starting statements with "You . . ." is a very good way to interrupt effective communication. Do you think you might be more open to listening if the above statements were rephrased to, "I feel mad because . . . ," "I didn't like what you did" or "I have a different opinion"?

It's true, of course, that you can start arguments with "I," but if your purpose is to state your opinion, your belief or your feeling, you will considerably increase the chances that your listener will be able to hear what you want to say if you make an "I" statement.

"I" statements that are direct, honest and sincere will multiply the possibilities for effective communication. Certainly, they can be aggressive if the speaker's intent is to be domineering, autocratic and blaming. If that's the intent, there's no technique that will prevent poor communication.

Phrases to Avoid in Communicating

The women in the groups have come up with an interesting list of "least helpful communication phrases."

1. You shouldn't feel that way.
2. That isn't important.
3. That doesn't exist.
4. I know I'm *right.*
5. Children should be seen and not heard.
6. Keep your thoughts to yourself.
7. If you ignore the situation, it will improve.
8. It will all work out.
9. Familiarity breeds contempt.
10. What you don't know won't hurt you.
11. Silence is golden.
12. If you love me, you should just know.
13. Shut up!

Importance of Humor in Communication

That list of phrases to avoid reminds me of one last important characteristic that you can cultivate to enrich your communication: your sense of humor.

There are numerous books in print today that present, with a lot of supporting evidence, the hypothesis that humor can help cure serious illnesses. I believe that hypothesis, but aside from that viewpoint, we all know

we just plain like to be around people who view life posi-
tively, who can see the humor in the situation and who
are able to laugh at themselves.

I do not mean sarcasm or teasing. Both of these
actions can frequently express anger or envy. Nor do I
mean laughing at or belittling another. These behaviors are not funny.

Using your sense of humor, you can convey support, hope, affection and caring. The effort is not to
cover up life but instead to view life optimistically. A
sense of humor can smooth out the bumps. But without
a doubt, your most important communication tools will
be your self-awareness, your belief in your personal
rights, your self-management and your recognition of
your personal power. Then you can easily implement
effective communication.

Twenty-Three Communication Techniques

The following techniques will help you develop
effective communication methods.

1. Understand your fears.
2. Pay attention to your own feelings.
3. Be familiar with your own self-definitions.
4. Remind yourself that flexibility reflects high self-
   esteem. Avoid trying to establish extremes of
   right or wrong, fair or unfair, logical or illogical
   or any other extremes.
5. Acknowledge the feelings about a situation before you volunteer solutions for it.
6. Identify the definitions of qualitative words. Be
   on the alert for interpretations.
7. Use the state-repeat-confirm method.

8. Pay attention to body language, both yours and others'.
9. Be prompt with your assertions.
10. Avoid powerless manipulation.
11. Say what you mean and mean what you say. Be honest, direct and sincere.
12. Don't ask questions if you don't want answers.
13. Avoid mind reading, hints and assumptions.
14. Remember that communication is both talking and listening.
15. Ask for clarification.
16. Use assertive statements about what you want instead of criticisms.
17. In personal relationships, understand the symbols of love.
18. Maintain your personal power.
19. Use "I" messages.
20. Remember that it takes two to argue.
21. Use your sense of humor.
22. Accord respect to yourself and to others.
23. Reinforce and enjoy your high self-esteem.

Notes

1. Virginia Satir, *Peoplemaking* (Palo Alto, Calif.: Science and Behavior Books, 1972).

12

. . . .

Awareness, Choice

and Freedom

You have read and reread the words *high self-worth*. High self-worth is the basis for effectively living one's life. It is the foundation for connecting and self-actualization. Unfortunately, too many of us have learned and absorbed the feelings of low self-worth to such a degree that it seems almost impossible to change. Quite the contrary is true. It is possible to choose, reinforce and enjoy high self-worth. Low self-worth is what frequently keeps people in intolerable circumstances. They don't comprehend or believe they have personal rights. They haven't learned how to be assertive. They are ignorant of possibilities to change, or resources to which they have access.

I'm not blind to the realities of economic dependency, racial and sexual discrimination, abusive mates, delinquent children, alcoholic relatives, aggressive colleagues, dependent children or parents and manipulative communication. I recognize the fears of loss, the tensions of sexual conflict and the struggle to establish one's own values and principles for living.

Yet, at the heart of these problems lies the feeling of low self-worth that results in feeling victimized and immobilized, blaming others or the system, and choosing to remain in a victimized position. This is a choice. You can choose to blame and do nothing. Or, you can choose high self-worth.

The Caught Caretaker Revisited

Throughout this book you have read repeatedly about the caught caretaker. Well, she's pretty devious, so it's important to watch for her. After all, the role is reinforced in girls, young women and older women. As you know, there are well-established behaviors for us as women. Many of these established ways warrant our challenging them so that we can determine whether they are working for us now. "It's always been that way" is not a good reason to continue destructive behavior.

A caught caretaker is a destructive person, not only to those around her, but also to herself. In fact, she is perhaps destructive to herself most of all, because everyone else has a chance to escape. If she chooses to not examine her behavior, she will suffer guilt and fear and anger, seeing herself as an innocent victim. She will not comprehend that rejection has anything to do with her manipulative communication. She will see herself as only loving and caring.

If you have someone in your life who is caught in her caretaker role, there is no need for you to reject her. Even though the possibility that she will change may seem remote, you can still care about her, love her.

How can you do that? By acknowledging your own personal power. Then you will have no desire to change her, or convince her that your point of view is the right one. You will not require that she understand or accept your life-style or opinions. By assertively claiming your personal rights, you can establish yourself as an individual apart from, yet connected to, those who are important to you. You can enhance your belief in yourself by practicing assertive communication techniques and self-management skills.

As a woman who believes in herself, you firmly acknowledge that you are the most important person in your life. You know that you will do things that you are proud of and also things that you wish you had not done. You understand that life cannot be without conflicts, external and internal, and that you will have growth to experience, no matter how old you are.

You are in charge of yourself. You understand that to blame is fruitless and to feel victimized is deadly. You comprehend that there are injustices and inequalities in your life and everyone else's, and you do what you can, and choose, to help yourself and others.

Choices and Creativity

Throughout this book, you have read the words *choice* and *choose*. With creativity, choices are our new options—options that perhaps you have never considered. Operating within the framework of a regulated (lawful) society, you still have many options for your behavior. You can learn by understanding, but to gain from that experience, it's very important to allow yourself to consider new definitions and opinions. Then you can choose what you want to do differently or keep the same. The only boundary you can impose on yourself is to limit your creativity and your options.

Creativity can be defined as the ability to consider old things in a new way, to produce something or enact new behavior that you hadn't considered or that hadn't been an option before. It can mean combining two seemingly dissimilar behaviors or ideas in a totally innovative fashion.

Why do we limit our creative thinking and our options? Sometimes it may be because it's easier to do things the way we've always done them, to follow the old routines. Perhaps it's because we procrastinate, trying to be perfect or correct or right, until there's no time to conceive an alternative. It could be that the way we've always done it seems to work. Even if something is boring and limiting, at least it's familiar; there aren't too many surprises.

Most often, however, we limit ourselves to old behaviors because we're fearful. We're afraid to be different. We're apprehensive about trying new behaviors or taking risks. We don't want to be criticized or condemned or thought of as difficult. We're frightened of losing our image or our old self-definition, or of having an image that stands out. We buy into the way it *should* be and are simply afraid of not being able to do it right.

We set our parameters of experience, constrain our curiosity and our search for self-awareness and allow ourselves to feel low self-esteem. As a result, our fears are magnified. We try to fit ourselves into rigid little boxes of definitions of how to live our lives. We do these things to ourselves. We cannot assign responsibility to men, our parents, our families, our jobs or to society in general.

Your creativity is how you think and feel about

things, how you combine your feelings and your thoughts to make choices and initiate new behaviors. Creativity is long-term thinking. Creativity thrives when you develop the skill to consider the whole picture instead of small parts.

Of course, we can't ignore the realities of life by irrationally expounding creativity and choices. Creativity alone won't make poverty go away, and choices aren't so apparent when we lack the skills to be economically independent. But we can believe in ourselves and we can search for new understandings and self-awareness. Maybe by doing that the realities won't seem so overwhelming.

People have some commonalities of behavior because of the society in which they live. Yet, each person is unique because of individual heritage and circumstances. We all have our own feeling–thinking–behavior wheel.

When you become aware of your feelings, when you understand your behavior, when you expand your choices and create new options, then you will experience freedom—freedom you may never have believed existed, freedom rooted in your self-management skills, your personal power and your high self-worth.

Postscript

I t's vital for each of you to lead your own life. You cannot live through others. You cannot be the tail on the kite. You *are* the kite—for yourself only.

You can love greatly, but you cannot have another be the central person for you, nor can you be the central person for another.

There's plenty of room for everyone. Set your goals and go for them.

About the Author

Darlene Deer Truchses is a psychotherapist in private practice in Denver, Colorado. She has developed the contents for this book through fifteen years of leading women's groups and private psychological counseling.

She has a B.A. in psychology and sociology and has done graduate work in counseling psychology. She is married to Dick Truchses, a clinical psychologist, with whom she works as a co-therapist. She has four children and eight grandchildren.